TWENTIETH
CENTURY
WORLD
HISTORY

AFRICA
IN THE
TWENTIETH
CENTURY

ELIZABETH CAMPLING

BATSFORD ACADEMIC AND EDUCATIONAL LIMITED LONDON

CONTENTS

ACKNOWLEDGMENT

The Author and Publishers thank the following for their kind permission to reproduce copyright illustrations: Africa Development for figs 41, 46; Associated Press for fig 53; Camera Press for figs 43, 44, 45, 47, 49; Camerapix for fig 52; Central Press for fig 54; Mary Evans Picture Library for fig 12; Ingelore Frank for fig 57; International Atomic Energy Agency for fig 25; International Labour Office for fig 37; Keystone Press Agency for fig 50; Mansell Collection for fig 21; Peter Newark for fig 11; Popperfoto for figs 3, 4, 5, 9, 15, 19, 23, 26, 27, 29, 30, 33, 35, 42, 51, 58; Rex Features Ltd for figs 36, 38, 55; John Topham Picture Library for figs 6, 7, 13, 14, 17, 20, 28, 31, 34, 39, 40, 48; United Nations for figs 22, 24. The maps were drawn by Alan Gunston. Picture research by Peta Hambling.

First published 1980
© Elizabeth Campling 1980

ISBN 0 7134 2492 3

Printed in Hong Kong
for the Publishers Batsford Academic and Educational Ltd,
4 Fitzhardinge Street, London W1H 0AH

THE COMING OF EUROPEAN RULE 1880-1900

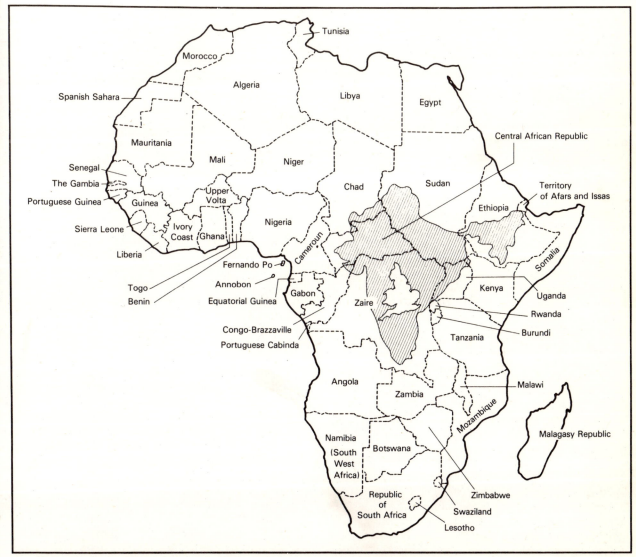

1 This map shows the immense size of the African continent, compared with the size of India (represented by the shaded area) and with the size of England and Wales (shown within the shaded area).

A VAST AND VARIED CONTINENT

By the late nineteenth century the size and geographical variety of the African continent (see pictures 1 and 2) — 5,000 miles from north to south and 2,000 miles wide at its narrowest point — had led to a great diversity of lifestyles, which make generalizations about "Africa" or "Africans" difficult. In distance, race and cultural experience, an Arab from the Maghrib in the north was as far removed from a West African negro or a South African Bantu, as a Laplander is from a Turk.

THE PEOPLES OF AFRICA IN 1880

The northern third of Africa was dominated by the Muslim religion. Here, between the seventh and the eighteenth centuries, the coastal belt and the Nile Valley boasted brilliant centres of Islamic learning, such as Cairo and Tripoli, and controlled a network of trade routes across the Sahara, which brought the salt, ivory and gold of the Sahel (see picture 2) to the Mediterranean markets. When the French occupied Algiers in 1830, they found that the majority of citizens were better educated than most Frenchmen. South of the coastal strip, the less sophisticated nomadic Berbers of the Sahara and the Fulani and Hausa pastoralists of the Sahel shared a common Islamic heritage, which gave them a sense of dignity and independence not easily suppressed by foreign rule.

The negroes of Equatorial and Central Africa shared no such common heritage. Contact with European traders, who sought slaves (until the slave-trade was outlawed in the mid-nineteenth century), ivory and rubber, had devastated some societies and benefitted others. States such as Dahomey and Ashanti had grown powerful by acting as commercial middlemen — procuring the produce required by Europeans and receiving, in return, firearms and consumer goods. A similar process of the survival of the fittest affected the Southern Savannah and East Africa. Here, the kingdoms of the Luba and the Lunda peoples in Katanga, and the kingdom of Buganda on the shores of Lake Victoria prospered by providing slaves for Portuguese and Arab slave-traders. This practice was still con-

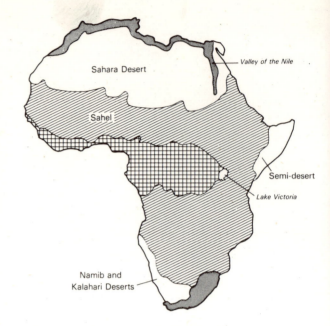

2   **The main geographical variations of Africa.**

Map labels: Sahara Desert; Valley of the Nile; Sahel; Semi-desert; Lake Victoria; Namib and Kalahari Deserts

Legend:

Mediterranean or temperate climate — suitable for growing citrus fruits, vines, wheat, etc.

Savannah or grassland — suitable for grazing and cultivation of cereals such as millet and maize. Unpredictable rainfall makes farming a hazardous proposition

Desert or semi-desert — suitable only for nomadic grazing

Equatorial and tropical forest — unsuitable for large-scale farming, but a source of tropical products such as rubber

tinuing when Livingstone made his missionary journeys in the mid-nineteenth century. Such kingdoms were often wealthy and sophisticated. In 1906 the German explorer, Leo Froebinius, wrote of a Lunda kingdom:

> There was not a man who did not carry sumptuous weapon of iron or copper, with inlaid hilts and damascened blades. Everywhere there were velvets and silken stuffs. Every cup, every pipe, every spoon was a piece of artistry, fully worthy of comparison with the creations of Europe.

Angola, on the other hand, was so depopulated by the slave-trade that it remains under-inhabited today.

In southern Africa the nineteenth-century expansion of white settlement from the Cape likewise caused upheavals among the native peoples. With the coming of the white men, the

3   A Basuto man. Before 1880 the people of Basutoland lived a peaceful, independent, pastoral life.

stone-age Bushmen had retreated to a life of hunting and gathering in the Namib and Kalahari deserts. The Bantu tribes had either been incorporated into the white man's state as mineworkers or farm labourers, or had preserved their identity by forming new tribes. The Zulus and the Matabele had developed into formidable military powers, and a Zulu army had annihilated a British one at Isandhlwana in 1879. In 1880 the Zulu nation was crushed, but the Matabele remained unconquered. The peoples of Bechuanaland, Basutoland (see picture 3) and

Swaziland maintained a peaceful, independent, pastoral lifestyle.

By 1880 no African people had reached the level of technical expertise acquired by Europe during the nineteenth-century Industrial Revolution.

AFRICA AND THE OUTSIDE WORLD BEFORE 1880

Until the 1880s contacts between Africans and non-Africans were restricted. There were British

and French trading posts on the west coast; Arab slave-traders operated from Zanzibar in the east; and isolated missionaries were active in central and eastern Africa. The missionaries' aim was not only to convert the Africans to Christianity, but also to regenerate African societies destroyed by the slave-trade and to establish "centres of civilization, for the promotion of true religion, agriculture and lawful commerce".

Only 10 per cent of the African continent was under direct European control. 276,000 Frenchmen had settled in Algeria since 1830, while in southern Africa four white-ruled states existed uneasily together. These were Cape Province and Natal, both part of the British Empire, and the Transvaal and the Orange Free State, founded by descendants of Dutch settlers, called the Boers. They spoke a dialect called Afrikaans, and were a frugal, fiercely religious farming people, who believed in the God-given supremacy of the white man over the black. In 1880 the leading Boer personality was Paul Kruger, President of the Transvaal. He was dedicated to protecting the purity of the Boer lifestyle from all outside influences.

Portugal claimed vast colonies in Angola and Mozambique but had little effective control over

6

4   Pretoria in the Transvaal, home of the Boers, at the end of the nineteenth century.

these areas, which were exploited through African middlemen. There were small British and French colonies on the west coast in Sierra Leone and Senegal.

THE SCRAMBLE 1880 - 1900

However, by 1900 most of Africa was ruled by six European powers — Belgium, Portugal, France, Italy, Great Britain and Germany. Historians still dispute the causes of the "Scramble" for colonies, but perhaps the most significant point is that the European governments acquired African territory less out of an interest in the continent itself, than out of a "dog in the manger" attitude. Each European power was afraid that its rivals would keep the trade of their new colonies to themselves. And so each power felt it had to enter the scramble, in order to reserve the largest possible area for its own future activities. Ambitious European traders, such as Karl Peters of the German East Africa Company, often pressurized their home government into action. The British South African millionaire, Cecil Rhodes, dreamt of carving a continuous band of British territory from the Cape to Cairo, and between 1889 and 1899 the Prime Minister, Lord Salisbury, allowed Rhodes' British South Africa Company to annex all the territory between Bechuanaland and Tanganyika.

Few European politicians had any knowledge of the territories they were acquiring. Lord Salisbury told a London audience:

> We have been engaged in drawing lines upon maps where no white man's foot has ever trod; we have been giving away mountains and rivers and lakes to each other, hindered only by the small impediment that we never knew exactly where they were.

5 A sitting of the native court at Mochudi in the British protectorate of Bechuanaland. Mochudi was the principal telegraph station of the British South Africa Company, but missionary influence had succeeded in excluding company influence from other areas of Bechuanaland life.

THE OCCUPATION

In 1884 the European powers met in Berlin to draw up an agreement on the division of Africa. It was decided that any claim for an area must be supported by the establishment of effective authority in the area concerned. The actual methods of occupation varied with personality and circumstance.

Some African peoples, aware of their backwardness in the face of European technology, asked for protectorate status. That is, they would accept foreign rule in return for protection against outside interference. They hoped thus to avoid conquest by an army or a concessionary company. For example, threatened with incorporation in the British South Africa Company's domain, the Bechuana chief, Khama, visited Queen Victoria in London in 1895 and begged to be allowed to become "a flea in the Queen's blanket".

Some African chiefs, ignorant of European legal procedures, were persuaded by trickery to

sign away their territory. This method was practised in the Congo by King Leopold of the Belgians, and in Equatorial Africa by the French. The most despicable example occurred however, in Matabeleland, where in 1889, Cecil Rhodes extracted from King Lobengula a concession allowing the British South Africa Company sole rights to prospect for minerals in Matabele territory. The concession was then used as a basis for complete occupation of the territory by 1893. When Lobengula realized that he had been tricked, he dispatched to London two venerable counsellors (Indunas), with a letter to Queen Victoria:

Lobengula can only find out the truth by sending eyes to see whether there is a Queen. The Indunas are his eyes. . . . He is much troubled by white men who come to his country and ask to dig gold. A document was written and presented to me for signature. About three months afterwards I heard from other sources that I had given the right to all the minerals in my country . . . I write to you that you may know the truth . . . . and not be deceived.

Lobengula's plea was unsuccessful.

THE SYSTEMS OF EUROPEAN RULE

No European government wanted to use its own funds to maintain colonies and all sought to make their African territories "self-sufficient". One method of cheap administration of a colony was to grant concessions to private companies, allowing them to exploit a particular area, in exchange for their undertaking to maintain law and order and to keep the national flag flying there. All four German colonies (Tanganyika, South West Africa, Togoland and Cameroons) and also Nigeria, Kenya and Rhodesia were governed by this method. Police duties were performed by private armies, such as the British South Africa Company Police or the West African Frontier Force.

Missionaries, fearing the effects of rapacious company-rule, often arranged for favoured tribes to acquire protectorate status, whereby their traditional lifestyle could be preserved, under European supervision. The Church of Scotland

Mission saved Nyasaland from incorporation into Rhodes' domain, and the Anglican missionaries at the court of the Kabaka (ruler) of Buganda achieved the same for Uganda in 1891. Khama's 1895 visit to London (see page 7) was undertaken on missionary advice.

Conscious of national dignity, the French and Italian governments were more greatly involved in the conquest of colonies than the British. From 1887 the Italian government sponsored settlement in Eritrea, while conquest of West Africa was undertaken by the French army. The Congo Free State was annexed by the Belgian King Leopold to his private estate and exploited by his own commercial company.

THE EXCEPTIONS

In 1879 bankrupt Egypt was taken over by a consortium of European financial experts from countries to whom Egypt owed money. In 1881 Egyptian army officers under Colonel Arabi Pasha rebelled and threatened to expel all foreigners. While other powers hesitated, Britain invaded Egypt in 1882 and defeated Arabi Pasha. Although the British remained thereafter officially only as advisers to the Khedive's government, their control in Egypt increased insidiously.

The Boer Republics, the Transvaal and the Orange Free State, resisted incorporation by defeating British forces at Majuba Hill in 1881. But Rhodes' determination to annex the two territories was only increased by the discovery of rich gold deposits at Witwatersrand in the Transvaal, and the two republics were finally annexed by the British government in 1902.

By 1902 only Ethiopia, Libya and Morocco remained free. Ethiopia had a two-thousand-year history as an independent kingdom with a distinctive Coptic Christian church. Two capable nineteenth-century emperors, Theodorous and Menelik, had overcome tribal disunity and created a unified state and an army equipped with modern firearms, mainly imported from Italy. In 1896 this army became the only African force to inflict a serious defeat on a European power, by annihilating the Italian army at Adowa. Not only did Ethiopia preserve her independence; she was herself able to take part in the "Scramble" by seizing the Muslim Ogaden region.

RESISTANCE TO EUROPEAN RULE

6 Cecil Rhodes visiting British soldiers during the Boer War in 1900. He was determined to annex the Boer republics, so that the British South Africa Company could exploit their gold and other minerals.

Some Africans resisted the initial invasion of their territory. This occurred particularly in areas with a strong sense of local or cultural pride or with a history of military glory. Muslims in the Sahel, under Samori, resisted French occupation until 1898. The Egyptian dependency of the Sudan defied British rule, under the leadership of a Muslim prophet, the Mahdi, whose fanatical army of "Dervishes" or "Fuzzy-Wuzzies" were eventually defeated at Omdurman in 1898.

Peoples who at first accepted European rule became disillusioned, and this often led to resistance later. Chiefs such as Lobengula felt cheated and sought revenge. Others, who had signed treaties with Europeans as equals, were shocked to encounter racial prejudice. Disruption of traditional lifestyles often brought resentment to boiling-point. The Ashanti of the Gold Coast rebelled in 1900, when the Governor, Sir Frederick Hodgson, demanded that they surrender the Golden Stool, symbol of Ashanti kingship. The Matabele rose twice — in 1893 and 1896. During the first war Lobengula died of European-imported smallpox.

In all cases, African resistance was crushed by the weight of superior European technology. Hillaire Belloc wrote a satirical couplet:

The difference is that we have got
The maxim gun, and they have not.

Psychological factors also played a part, as future Rhodesian nationalist leader, Ndabaningi Sithole has testified:

The African was simply overwhelmed, overawed, perplexed, mystified and dazzled. . . . Mines were opened throughout the country. The dynamite that exploded the huge rocks confirmed the belief that the white man was

9

7 African and European workers and their families at a diamond mine in Kimberley, South Africa, in the 1880s.

a god . . . (possessing) all power, wealth, skills and knowledge. The African, who never argues with his gods, lest their wrath visit him, adopted the same attitude to the white man.

Rarely did rival tribes unite in opposition to the Europeans. Indeed, Europeans were often able to gain territory, at small cost to themselves, by exploiting tribal feuds and allying with one African group against another. For example, during the British occupation of Uganda (which was formed from an amalgamation of Buganda, Toro and Bunyoro Kingdoms), Bunyoro was conquered on behalf of Britain by the Bugandans, Bunyoro's old rivals. Or, again, the Matabele refused to join forces with their old enemy, the Mashona, against Rhodes' South Africa Company, until the 1896 rebellion was on the verge of defeat.

YOUNG HISTORIAN

A

1 Which African societies prospered in the nineteenth century? Why were they able to achieve this?

2 To what extent were Europeans involved in Africa before 1880? Give an account of the different types of involvement.

3 Explain the sudden European interest in Africa in about 1880, as it might have been seen by (a) a European prime minister, (b) a trader with interests in Africa.

4 By what methods did Europeans gain control in Africa? Under which system do you think that Africans came off best?

5 What effects on the colonization of Africa were achieved by (a) missionaries, (b) trading companies?

6 Why was African resistance to European conquest so futile? Were there any exceptions to this rule, and if so, explain why they occurred?

B

Write the letters which might have been sent by the following:

1 A visitor to North Africa in 1870.

2 A missionary in Katanga in about 1870.

3 A Boer, commenting on British policy in about 1880.

4 Karl Peters to Bismarck (the German Chancellor) urging the annexation of Tanganyika.

5 A missionary in Bechuanaland, watching the activities of Cecil Rhodes in southern Africa.

C

Write the headlines which might have appeared in (a) a pro-colonial and (b) an anti-colonial newspaper on the following occasions:

1 The Zulu victory at Isandhlwana.

2 The visit of chief Khama to London in 1895.

3 The defeat of Arabi Pasha.

4 The visit of Lobengula's Indunas to London.

5 The defeat of the Italians at Adowa.

6 The battle of Omdurman.

D

1 On an outline map of Africa, sketch in the main racial groups.

2 Design posters for the following: (a) The German Colonial Society, (b) the British South Africa Company, (c) The Italian government's campaign to encourage emigration to Eritrea.

THE COLONIAL PERIOD 1900-1914 1

Picture 8 shows the countries of Africa in 1900, with their colonial rulers.

THE NEW RULERS

European governments believed that their main duty in Africa was to maintain law and order, and to do so at the expense of the colony, not of the European taxpayer. Little importance was attached to the education and welfare of the new subjects — such concerns were better left to private enterprise and the missions. Even the act of governing was often left to chartered companies, although by 1900 both the German and Imperial East Africa Companies in Tanganyika and Kenya respectively had found that this put too great a strain on their finances and had handed the responsibility for those countries back to the reluctant home governments. One of the few constructive activities undertaken in this era was the building of roads and railways into the interior, the more effectively to collect taxes and impose law and order.

THE ROOTS OF NATIONALISM

By 1900 the era of fierce resistance by African peoples defending their traditional lifestyles was over. The exceptions were the risings in Tanganyika and German South West Africa (see page 23). In time, a new form of nationalism was to arise among educated Africans, whose aim would not be to return to pre-colonial tribal life, but to gain acknowledgement of the Africans' right to administer for themselves the modern, European-imposed state. Before 1914 this phenomenon was evident only in the Muslim colonies of Egypt and Tunisia, where an educated class already existed.

EDUCATION

In the less advanced tropical colonies, the groundwork for a future generation of African nationalists was unwittingly laid by the proliferation of mission schools after 1900. These schools aimed only to give an elementary education in Christianity and the 3 Rs, but a small number of gifted pupils went on to train as preachers and teachers or even to study at European or American universities. The future Zambian president, Kenneth Kaunda, described such a school:

> The method of teaching young children . . . . was to gather them under a tree on which was hung a cloth painted with the letters of the alphabet. I well remember sitting for hours under a shady tree chanting a-e-i-o-u, then forming the letters with my fingers in the sand . . . . Each cloth was called Nsalu, and when we had Nsalu 1, 2 and 3, we were promoted to the first class, where we were allowed to use slates.

Before 1914 few Europeans took educated Africans seriously. They were referred to as "trousered blacks".

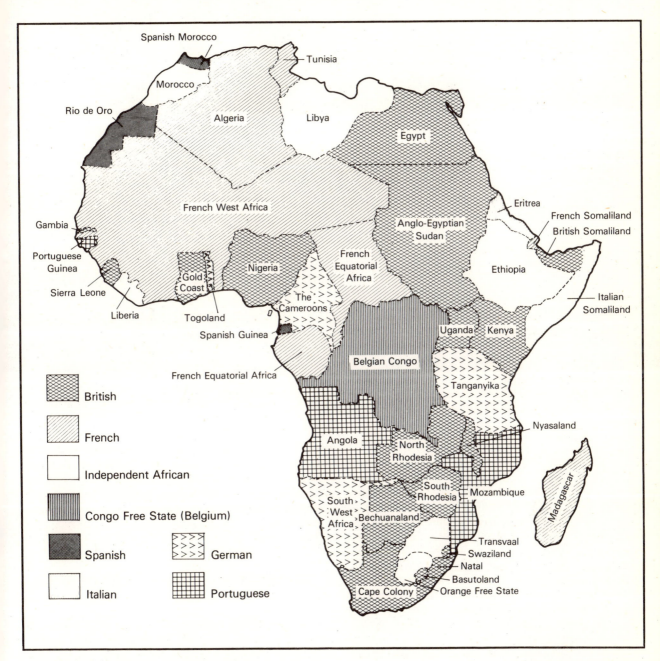

8　Colonial possessions in Africa in 1900.

Legend:

- British
- French
- Independent African
- Congo Free State (Belgium)
- Spanish
- German
- Italian
- Portuguese

Map labels: Spanish Morocco, Tunisia, Morocco, Algeria, Libya, Rio de Oro, Egypt, French West Africa, Anglo-Egyptian Sudan, Eritrea, French Somaliland, British Somaliland, Gambia, Portuguese Guinea, Sierra Leone, Liberia, Togoland, Gold Coast, Nigeria, French Equatorial Africa, The Cameroons, Ethiopia, Italian Somaliland, Spanish Guinea, French Equatorial Africa, Belgian Congo, Uganda, Kenya, Tanganyika, Nyasaland, Angola, North Rhodesia, South Rhodesia, Mozambique, Madagascar, South West Africa, Bechuanaland, Transvaal, Swaziland, Natal, Basutoland, Orange Free State, Cape Colony

"SELF-SUFFICIENCY"

Apart from by granting concessions (page 8), there were two alternative methods of making a colony self-supporting. Where a flourishing agriculture already existed, as in West Africa, African farmers were encouraged to grow just one or two "cash crops" which were commercially profitable. The profits made by exporting these could then be partially appropriated by the colonial government as taxation. They also paid for imports of necessary goods. The African farmers within such a cash-crop economy acquired some degree of independence and self-employment, but they were at the mercy of world fluctuations in demand, which could cause dramatic falls in their income. A further disadvantage of growing cash crops was that it

13

reduced the amount of land available for growing subsistence foodcrops. Even apparently prosperous colonies such as the Gold Coast needed to import food for people to eat.

In colonies where the climate was suitable, it was hoped that self-sufficiency could be induced by establishing white-owned estates (plantations). Humid West Africa, where the annual death-rate from fever among British officials in 1904 was 27.3 per cent, saw no permanent white settlement. But in Kenya, Southern Rhodesia and South West Africa, where the climate was cooler and drier, African land was confiscated, and a landless labouring class came into being, which was dependent on the whites for employment. The privileged lifestyle of the settlers — with its plentiful supply of cheap farm labour and domestic servants — bred in them a determination to preserve these advantages for future generations.

FRONTIERS AND TRIBES

Colonies were artificial creations, whose frontiers had first been drawn on paper by people who were in complete ignorance of tribal boundaries. Nigeria, Kenya and Northern

9 The Europeans built railways into the interior of Africa. Here people of the Masai tribe are at a station on the Kenya and Uganda Railway.

Rhodesia, in particular, encompassed mutually antagonistic tribes. Other African societies were split up by colonial frontiers. The Muslim Somalis were shared out between five areas: British, French and Italian Somaliland, Ethiopia and Kenya.

ASSIMILATION VERSUS INDIRECT RULE

French African territories were designated not as colonies, but as part of France d'Outremer (France Overseas). Tribes were broken up, chiefs deprived of their status and the French system of government imposed. The territories were divided into "departments", and each department sent deputies to the National Assembly in Paris. Africans who could read, write and speak French, who had done military service, worked for the French for ten years, and who had only one wife, were eligible for French citizenship, including enfranchisement (being given the right to vote). This was known as the policy of "assimilation".

14

Although, in theory, assimilation was based on racial equality, it remained, in practice, the privilege of the few Africans who could obtain an education or who were willing to reject their native culture. By 1926 only 50,722 West Africans out of a total of 13,499,000 had been assimilated. The privileged few were given prestigious jobs as interpreters, policemen and administrators in the interior and were often "more French than the French". Non-assimilated Africans were classed as "subjects"; although eligible for taxation, military service and forced labour, they had few political rights and were subject to the "Indigenat", a law which allowed French colonial officials to imprison without trial.

While the French followed their policy of assimilation, the British, outside the settler colonies, used the system of "indirect rule". Under this system, British residents in the colony supervised government by traditional chiefs. Although this method had a less destructive effect than assimilation on tribal life, it sometimes acted as a bar to economic and social progress, and customs such as slavery and polygamy were often tolerated. In the words of a Lieutenant-Governor of Nigeria in 1917:

> You must shut your eyes, up to a certain point, to a great many practices which, though not absolutely repugnant to humanity, are nevertheless reprehensible to our ideas. . . .
> You must have patience with the liar though he lies seventy times seven; you must at times have patience with the pecculator of public funds (a hard pill this to swallow).

Such a system, moreover, gave few opportunities in government to the educated Africans.

ALGERIA AND TUNISIA

As Muslim states, Algeria and Tunisia both possessed a cultured population in the coastal towns, while the desert interior was dominated by the fiercely independent Muslim Berbers.

Since 1830 Algeria had been fully assimilated with France, but few Arabs had abandoned Muslim for Christian law in order to become French citizens. Half a million French settlers or "colons" had settled in Algeria by 1914 and a small proportion of the wealthiest colons — comprising about 2 per cent of the Algerian population — owned one third of the country's limited amount of cultivable land. The colons doggedly defended their privileged position. "It is difficult," complained a French colonial minister, Jules Ferry, in 1892, "to try and convince the European settler that there are rights other than his own in Arab country and that the native is not a race to be taxed and exploited to the utmost limits."

In Tunisia, where there were 10,000 French settlers by 1914, there was open evidence of French contempt for Muslim traditions. The Wafq lands, which belonged to the Islamic Church and whose proceeds were used to endow Islamic schools and build mosques, were seized. Tunisia saw the rise of one of the first modern nationalist parties in colonial Africa — the Young Tunisia Party, led by Ali Bash Hamba.

EGYPT

Although the outward show of the Khedive's government in Egypt was maintained, the British influence, under "Chief Advisers" Lord Cromer (1883-1907), Sir Eldon Gorst (1907-11) and Lord Kitchener (1911-14), can best be seen in the words of a British Foreign Minister:

> It is essential that in important questions affecting the administration and safety of Egypt, the advice of Her Majesty's Government should be followed . . . . Ministers and Governors must carry out this advice or forfeit their offices.

Important economic reforms were achieved: the first Aswan Dam, completed in 1902, greatly increased the area of cultivable land in Egypt. Educated Egyptians, however, resented the loss of their freedom and the contributions Egypt was forced to make to the cost of British occupation. A Muslim nationalist party of doctors, lawyers and teachers developed in the late nineteenth century under Mustapha Kamil, and aimed at the expulsion of both the British and the Khedive. After an incident between Egyptians and British officers at Dinshawai in 1906, four Egyptians were publicly hanged and violence erupted. A ballad, "Egypt and Cromer", summed up popular feeling:

They fell upon Dinshawai
And spared neither man nor his brother,
Slowly they hanged the one and flogged
the other,
It was a gloomy day when Zahran was killed,
His mother from the roof watched, while
tears from her were spilled,
His brother, O you people, stood by him,
And gazed till his eyes grew dim.

The British response to nationalist agitation was repression.

FRENCH WEST AFRICA AND EQUATORIAL AFRICA

While French West Africa enjoyed a system of cash-crop agriculture, Equatorial Africa was surrendered in 1899 to forty companies with thirty-year concessions. French historians have dubbed this "the period of pillage" and claimed that the population were "so hard-hit they were never to recover".

Outside the coastal regions of Senegal, which elected Blaise Diagne the first black deputy to the French Assembly in 1914, assimilation remained a myth. With few educational facilities and a large number of rival tribes, there was little political awareness before 1914.

10   Barges laden with sacks of groundnuts on the river Gambia in the British colony of the Gambia. Groundnuts were grown as a cash-crop for exporting to Europe.

BRITISH WEST AFRICA

Indirect rule in British West Africa encouraged the perpetuation of tribal identities. As late as the 1950s the Ashanti remembered their days of independence and military glory. In northern Nigeria Muslim Emirs (chiefs) continued to rule, and tribal differences between Muslim Hausa and Fulani, on the one hand, and pagan and Christian Yoruba and Ibo, on the other (see picture 32), were accentuated by the exclusion of Christian mission schools from the north and the consequent gap in the standard of literacy between north and south.

European demand in the early twentieth century for rubber, gold, cocoa, groundnut oil (for soap) and timber brought prosperity to a considerable number of West African cash-crop farmers. By 1914 the value of the Gold Coast's gold exports had risen to £1,607,000 annually, while cocoa exports had reached a value of £2,194,000. Outside South Africa, the Gold Coast was the wealthiest colony. Partly for humanitarian reasons, and partly because the cash-crop economy worked so well, the British

11 Emperor Menelik of Ethiopia. He was the only African ruler to successfully resist European annexation.

government firmly opposed all plantation agriculture in West Africa. Lever Brothers' request to start a palm-oil plantation in Nigeria was refused.

ETHIOPIA

Until his death in 1912 Emperor Menelik continued his modernization work in Ethiopia, including the installation of telephones and electricity in the capital, Addis Ababa, the opening of the first public school and the mass vaccination of his subjects in 1898. However, political power remained firmly in the hands of a small class of Amharic-speaking nobles, and rule over non-Ethiopian subjects — the Somalis of the Ogaden and the pagan Galla in the south — remained oppressive.

MOROCCO AND LIBYA

By 1914 both Morocco and Libya had come under European rule. In 1911 the capital of Morocco, Fez, rose in rebellion, and Sultan Mulay Hafid accepted a French protectorate to preserve his throne. The aim of the first French "Resident", General Lyautey, differed radically from those of French Algerians and Tunisians:

> It is to be foreseen — and indeed I regard it as a historic truth — that in the more or less distant future North Africa — modernized, civilized, living its own autonomous life — will detach itself from metropolitan France. When this occurs — and it must be our supreme political goal — the parting must occur without pain and nations must be able to view France without fear.

All laws continued to be issued in the sultan's name and, at local level, power remained with

17

12 Heads of rebels on the Traitors' Gate at Fez, Morocco, 1911. The rebellion provided the excuse for a total French takeover of Morocco.

the traditional Muslim dignitaries, the Caids.

Economic progress was impressive. A large artificial harbour was built at Casablanca and a network of roads constructed to assist the transport of peasant produce to the coastal markets. As elsewhere in the Maghrib, French control over the tribes of the interior — the Rifs — remained tenuous.

The Italian conquest of Libya, begun in 1912, was not completed until 1932. This was due to the fanatical resistance by Muslim Sanussi, who declared a "Jihad" or holy war in defence of their traditional way of life.

YOUNG HISTORIAN

A

1 Describe the system by which European governments tried to administer their colonies on the cheap. Why were some of these methods unsuccessful?
2 How would you define "nationalism"? Could it be said to have existed in Africa before the First World War?
3 What is the difference between a subsistence and a cash-crop economy? What are the advantages and disadvantages of the latter?
4 (a) Why was white settlement encouraged?
(b) Why was there more white settlement in some areas than in others?
(c) What advantages did the settlers gain?
(d) What disadvantages did the system bring to Africans?
5 Was the policy of assimilation "more of a myth than a reality"?
6 What were the disadvantages of the system of indirect rule?
7 Write a paragraph on each of the following: (a) the colons of Algeria, (b) the growth of nationalism in Egypt before 1914, (c) the different fates of Africans in the French and British West African colonies.

B

1 Write the letter which might have been sent by an assimilated French African, describing his life in the French colonial service.
2 Write the letter which might have been sent by a French visitor to Algeria in 1914, describing his impressions of the colony.
3 Write the letter which might have been sent by an educated Egyptian to a friend, justifying his attitude to British rule.
4 Write the letter which Lyautey might have sent to the government in Paris, justifying his policy in Morocco.

C

Write the headlines which might have appeared in (a) a pro-colonial, (b) an anti-colonial newspaper on the following occasions:
1 The affray at Dinshawai 1906.
2 The Italian invasion of Libya 1912.
3 The seizure of Wafq lands in Tunisia.
4 The election of Diagne to the French Assembly 1914.

D

1 Write the advertisement which might have been issued by the French government, encouraging settlers to emigrate to Algeria or Tunisia.
2 Write the anti-British pamphlet which might have been issued by Egyptian nationalists in 1906-7.

THE COLONIAL PERIOD 1900-1914 II: CENTRAL, EASTERN AND SOUTHERN AFRICA

CONGO FREE STATE

King Leopold of the Belgians annexed the Congo as his own private estate. A Belgian colonial lawyer said in 1906:

> The colony is administered neither in the interests of the natives, nor even in the economic interests of Belgium. To win a maximum revenue for the king: that is the regulator of its administrative action.

Leopold granted exploitation rights to concessionary companies such as the Katanga Company. The invention of the pneumatic tyre in 1888 had created a boom demand in Europe for rubber. In the interests of profits, the concessionary companies employed squads of armed men to coerce the unwilling natives into gathering rubber. In 1903 the abuses were revealed to the world by the British consul, Roger Casement. He quoted a villager's reply to the question: how much was he paid for rubber-picking:

> Our village got cloth and a little salt, but not the people who did the work. Our chiefs ate up the cloth; the workers got nothing . . . . It used to take ten days to get the twenty baskets of rubber — we were always in the forest, and then when we were late we were killed. We had to go farther and farther into

the forest to find the rubber vines . . . and our women had to give up cultivating the fields and gardens. Then we starved . . . we begged the white men to leave us alone, saying we could get no more rubber, but the white men and their soldiers said: "Go! You are only beasts yourselves."

In 1919 a Belgian committee estimated that the Congolese population was only half what it had been in 1880.

The public outcry in Belgium and elsewhere forced Leopold to hand over his state to the Belgian government in 1906. They renamed it the Belgian Congo. The practice of forced labour on plantations continued, although the worst abuses were eliminated.

UGANDA AND KENYA

The contrast in the treatment of these two territories is interesting. Missionary pressure had acquired protectorate status for Uganda. The state was to be run in the interests of the Africans, and white settlement was forbidden. The cooperative Bugandans were given a privileged position in the 1900 agreement:

> So long as the Kabaka, chiefs and people of Buganda shall conform to the laws and regulations instituted for their governance by Her Majesty's government . . . H. M. Govern-

20

13 Missionaries and natives show the amputated hands of men killed by the troops of the Congo Free State. When such abuses became known in Europe, a public outcry forced King Leopold of the Belgians to hand over the state to the Belgian government.

ment agrees to recognize the Kabaka as the native ruler of the Province of Uganda under H.M.Government's protection and overrule.

Buganda received priority treatment over Bunyoro and Toro in any schemes of improvement and her capital, Kampala, became the capital of Uganda.

In Kenya, disappointed at the Imperial East Africa Company's failure to meet its obligations to maintain law and order and at the unprofitability of the publicly financed Kenya railway, the British government left much initiative to the first High Commissioner, Sir Charles Eliot. He saw white plantation agriculture as the solution for creating a viable economy. In 1902 a traveller, Colonel Meinertzhagen, interviewed Eliot in Nairobi:

He envisaged a thriving colony of thousands of Europeans with their families, the whole of the country from the Aberdares and Mount Kenya to the German border . . . divided up into farms . . . . He intended to confine the natives to reserves and use them as cheap labour for farms.

I suggested that the country belonged to the Africans and that their interests must prevail over the interests of strangers. He would not have it . . . . I said that some day the African would be educated and armed; that would lead to a clash. Eliot thought that that day was so far distant as not to matter.

By 1915 4.5 million acres of fertile land in Kenya had been expropriated from two pastoral tribes, the Kikuyu and the Masai, to form the White Highlands, an exclusively European farming reserve. Africans were herded into native reserves, composed of poor-quality land without the capacity to absorb a rising population.

14 A German caricature of King Leopold of the
Belgians, drawn in 1905.

TANGANYIKA

Infested by tse-tse fly and with few marketable
crops or minerals, the German East African
colony of Tanganyika seemed the least promising of all territories. The German doctrine
that colonies must "pay their own way" (even
the building of such basic facilities as railways
was left to private enterprise) was such a failure
that the desperate Tanganyikan administration
introduced the forced cultivation of cash-crops
such as sisal (similar to hemp) and coffee. The
profits were to finance the government.

There were over 120 tribes in Tanganyika,
few of them having more than one million
members, but, against all the odds, they rose in
united opposition to the government's harsh
policy. The "Maji-Maji" rising of 1905-06 was
named from the Swahili word for water; witch-
doctors had assured the rebels that European
bullets would turn harmlessly to water. The
Germans subdued the rising ruthlessly, des-
troying African crops in an attempt to starve the
rebels into surrender. It is estimated that
between 70,000 and 80,000 died.

15 A Basutoland diamond digger in front of his
diamond mine. In the background are police tents. The
three protectorates could only survive economically by
supplying cheap labour to the South African mines.

GERMAN SOUTH WEST AFRICA

The Namib and Kalahari deserts make much of
South West Africa uninhabitable, suitable only
for a nomadic, pastoral life. It was not until
1908 that the first diamond deposits were
discovered. Hopes to make German South West
Africa self-sufficient rested on exploitation by
chartered companies and on immigration. By
1903 nine companies controlled one third of the
country and 12,000 German settlers had arrived,
encroaching on the traditional grazing lands of
the two major tribes, the Ovambo and Herero.

In 1904 the Herero rebelled. Arriving from
Germany with 15,000 troops, General Trotha
regarded the rebellion as an opportunity to
exterminate the Herero as a race:

The Hereros must leave the land. If they
refuse I shall compel them with the gun. I
shall assume charge of no more women and

23

children, but shall drive them back to their people or let them be shot at.

Two thirds of the tribe were killed, their lands confiscated and cattle-owning forbidden; the survivors were forced to become labourers on European farms.

Events in Tanganyika and South West Africa provoked a crisis of conscience in Germany. The Reichstag (German Parliament) strongly criticized the government. A colonial minister, Dernburg, was appointed and the Reichstag granted loans for the construction of railways and the introduction of new crops. Culpable colonial governors were replaced. However, in the seven years remaining to Germany as a colonial power, little was actually achieved in economic reconstruction, railway-building or education. The chief legacy of German colonialism was the destruction of tribal life in South West Africa.

THE PORTUGUESE EMPIRE
MOZAMBIQUE, ANGOLA AND GUINEA

The "Scramble" (page 6) provoked Portugal to reassess her hitherto casual attitude towards her territories. Dos Santos, a Portuguese historian, wrote in 1903:

> We did not know and we do not know how to colonize . . . . We are utopian dreamers, a race of inept sluggards, who have always been content with national sovereignty.

Military action had brought Angola and Mozambique under control by 1909. Desperately poor herself, Portugal was unable to amass sufficient funds to develop her colonies and encouraged foreign investors to provide capital for building railways and opening mines. By 1911 half of Mozambique was controlled by concessionary companies. Although humanitarian legislation was passed in Lisbon, in practice, forced labour was condoned, especially after the discovery of diamonds in Angola. The Governor of Mozambique justified the system:

> Still I do not understand by what moral or legal doctrine our metropolitan legislators can justify their scruples in not obliging the half-savage African to work for himself and his society.

24

Although educated Africans were eligible for Portuguese citizenship, the majority remained "Indigenas" (non-citizens), unprotected by law and vulnerable to exploitation. Little interest was shown by the Portuguese authorities in African education. Even the mission schools were closed when the Jesuits were expelled for criticizing the government.

RHODESIA AND NYASALAND

Frustrated in its search for minerals in Rhodesia and Nyasaland, the British South Africa Company encouraged white settlement there. By 1914 10,000 Britons and Afrikaners had arrived in the southern area of Rhodesia, where the shattered and decimated Matabele population were systematically herded into reserves. By 1914 Africans occupied only 22 per cent of former Matabele territory. A battle for survival drove Africans to seek employment on European farms, and their freedom of movement was restricted by Pass Laws. These made it legally binding on an African to be in possession of a special pass before he could enter a white area.

The British government made only spasmodic attempts to counter the worst excesses of company rule. In 1901 Colonial Secretary, Joseph Chamberlain ordered an investigation into the coercion of Rhodesian Africans into labour on white farms, but the Commission's report was never acted on.

Rhodesia's communications with the outside world were improved by company-financed railway-building. Landlocked Rhodesia was now linked to the Indian Ocean at Beira in Mozambique. In other respects, however, this colony appeared to be an economic failure. The fabled gold deposits did not materialize. White immigration fell far below the levels anticipated and the Matabele did not make docile labourers.

Mission influence and a shortage of white settlers protected the northern half of Rhodesia from the worst excesses of company rule. Extensive copper deposits were not discovered until after the concession had expired in 1923. Tribal life here was therefore less disrupted and the majority of Africans maintained a simple subsistence agriculture.

All white settlement was banned in mission-protected Nyasaland (see page 8). However,

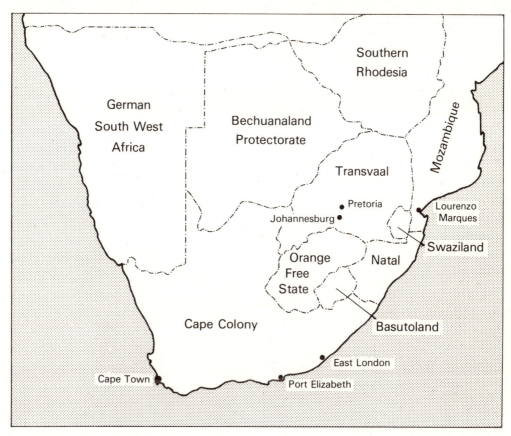

poverty compelled many Nyasa to migrate to the South African gold mines. In Nyasaland contact with a more sophisticated society and the prevalence of mission schools produced the first modern nationalist movement in southern Africa. In 1912 a group of educated Nyasa founded the Northern Nyasaland Nationalist Association, which agitated for African representation on the legislative council.

SOUTH AFRICA

The conflict of interest between British and Boers in South Africa erupted in 1899, when the British High Commissioner, Sir Alfred Milne, deliberately provoked the gold-rich Transvaal so as to make an excuse for annexation. After some astounding initial successes, the main Boer army was defeated in 1900, although guerillas or "commandos" continued the fight for a further two years. The British army was ill-equipped to deal with "these Boers who sit quietly at home one day and fire at British troops the next". Kitchener's armies fenced off areas of the veldt,

16   South Africa at the time of the Boer War.

17   British soldiers in the Boer War.

the high grasslands of South Africa, and scoured each one systematically, burning any farm that might shelter commandos, and housing women and children in "concentration camps". Inevitable injustices followed. The camps were inefficiently run and many died of disease or malnutrition. A British officer described how indiscriminate the burning of farms could be:

Farm-burning goes merrily on, and our course through the country is marked as in pre-historic ages by pillars of smoke by day and fire by night . . . . I do not gather that any special reason or purpose is alleged or proved against the farms burnt. If the Boers have used the farm, if the owner is on commando, if the line within a certain distance has been blown up, or even if there are Boers in the neighbourhood who persist in fighting — these are some of the reasons . . . . Anyway . . . one reason or another generally covers pretty nearly every farm we come to, and so to save trouble we burn the lot of them without enquiry.

In 1902 the peace treaty of Vereeniging was signed. The Boers became British citizens, with a promise of self-government in the future. A Boer condition, that no political rights be given to black Africans in either the Transvaal or the Orange Free State, was agreed.

In the 1907 elections Boer parties won a majority in every state in South Africa except Natal. In the two former Boer Republics, the Transvaal and the Orange Free State, Het Volk (later the South Africa Party) was led by former commando generals, Botha and Smuts. Throughout the nineteenth century the Boers had shunned British rule for fear that their doctrine of white supremacy would be weakened. But in 1909 they consented to join the two British South African colonies in a self-governing dominion, the Union of South Africa, confident that they could dominate it. The constitution of the dominion, instituted in 1910, was slanted to favour Boer ideas: no non-white could vote for the federal parliament in Pretoria and rural constituencies were given a disproportionately large number of seats.

Not all Afrikaners — as the Boers were now coming to be called — accepted the Union of South Africa with optimism. Hertzog, a leading Het Volk politician, argued that cooperation with English-speaking South Africans would dilute the purity of Afrikanerdom, and in 1913

he formed a breakaway Nationalist Party.

Many historians now argue that too much attention is paid to the conflict between the British and Boer whites; the Boer War was less significant in the long run than the common attitude of whites towards blacks that was typified in the Treaty of Vereeniging. From 1900 the remaining rights of Africans were gradually eroded. In 1913 a Land Act forbade African ownership of land in 90 per cent of South Africa. To labour on white farms was the only alternative for the Africans, which placed them under a paternalistic regime in which the farm-owner had the right to intervene even in domestic quarrels. Pass Laws were enacted. Dispossessed Africans, driven to work in mines, were forced to leave their families and lodge in bachelor dormitories run by the mining companies. The expansion of the mining industry also attracted more whites to the urban areas, and white miners were determined to preserve the better-paid, more highly-skilled jobs for themselves. It was doubtful whether any South African government that did not enforce white supremacy could survive.

Although Africans outnumbered whites by 4 to 1, there was little resistance. Tribal life had been shattered in the nineteenth century and a generation of chiefs destroyed. The new chiefs had been appointed by the government for their docility. Moreover, the Zulu, Xhosa, Ponda, etc, failed to unite their protests. Only in Cape Province did Africans participate in political life. There, the nineteenth-century "colour-blind" constitution enabled some blacks to receive an education. In 1912 an opposition movement, the African National Congress (ANC), was founded to campaign for political equality for all races. To succeed, however, it would need to attract support from chiefs and exploited labourers and overcome tribal rivalries.

The three "fleas in the Queen's blanket" (the British protectorates) were saved from incorporation in the Union of South Africa by the protection of the British government, who insisted that incorporation should not occur until a majority of the inhabitants consented. All three, however, were economically dependent on South Africa: Swaziland and Basutoland, entirely surrounded by South African territory, and suffering from chronic over-population and soil erosion, survived primarily as a labour reserve for the Witwatersrand mines in the Transvaal; Bechuanaland supplied beef cattle for the same market.

YOUNG HISTORIAN

A

1 Compare the attitudes towards their colonies of Germany, Portugal and Britain.

2 In what areas did Europeans settle? Describe the attitude of the settlers towards the native population in two of these areas.

3 What important wars and rebellions occurred in southern and eastern Africa? Give an account of two of these, describing (a) the participants, (b) the issues at stake, (c) the results.

4 Give an account of the role of missionaries in southern and eastern Africa before 1914, using examples from as many areas as possible.

5 Why is it often said that the Boers "lost the war but won the peace"?

6 In 1906 a fierce debate took place over Africa in the German parliament (the Reichstag). (a) What was the occasion of this debate? (b) What were its results? (c) In what other European state did a similar course of events occur?

B

Compose the letters which might have been written by the following:

1 A Boer farmer in 1902, describing his attitude towards the British government.

2 A British or French reporter in the Congo, to his editor in 1900.

3 A missionary in Kenya, on relations between the settlers and the native population.

4 The wife of a farmer in Southern Rhodesia, on the advantages and the disadvantages of life in the colony.

C

Compose the newspaper headlines which might have appeared on the following occasions:

1 The 1906 debate on German colonial policy.

2 The publication of Casement's report from the Congo.

3 The outbreak of the Boer War in (a) a British newspaper, (b) an Afrikaner newspaper.

D

Few Africans were literate in 1914, but how might the following, writing in the 1920s, have remembered their childhoods:

1 A Boer born in 1895.

2 A Herero born in 1898.

3 A mission-educated Ugandan born in 1900.

4 The child of white Kenyan settlers born in 1900.

THE BIRTH OF NATIONALISM 1919-1939

THE IMPACT OF THE FIRST WORLD WAR

The main practical effect of the First World War on Africa was that Germany disappeared as a colonial power. The four German colonies were redistributed by the Treaty of Versailles as mandates under League of Nations supervision. South West Africa was mandated to the Union of South Africa, and Tanganyika to Britain (with a small area in the southwest going to Belgium as the new colony of Ruanda-Urundi). The Cameroons and Togoland were divided between France and Britain.

A deeper effect of the war was the psychological change it wrought in the attitudes of colonial governments and their white and Muslim subjects. The Covenant of the League of Nations laid down that "peoples not yet able to stand by themselves under the strenuous conditions of the modern world" should be placed under the "tutelage" of more advanced nations, for whom their well-being and development should form "a sacred trust of civilization". Although this principle legally applied only to the confiscated German colonies, it generated a greater sense of responsibility for the welfare of Africa in general. In 1922 the former Governor-General of Nigeria, Lord Lugard, published a book entitled *The Dual Mandate in Tropical Africa*, in which he stressed the Europeans' responsibility to steer their African subjects towards economic advancement and a limited degree of self-government. Influenced by the new atmosphere, the British government gave grants to mission-run elementary education and opened the first secondary schools to train doctors, teachers and agronomists.

EDUCATION

Education also expanded in the French and Belgian colonies, but according to very different principles. The aim of French education was to produce loyal, assimilated, black Frenchmen. All primary education was controlled by the colonial government, and secondary institutions such as the William Ponty School in Dakar were devoted exclusively to producing men for government service. The Belgians concentrated entirely on primary education, for reasons explained by a colonial minister in 1954:

> We have seen that those natives who have been shown Europe, and given a very advanced education, do not always return to their homelands in a spirit favourable to civilization and to the Mother Country in particular.

Whereas a tiny minority of French and British Africans studied abroad, such as Habib Bourguiba of Tunisia, Kwame Nkrumah of the Gold Coast and Nmandi Azikiwe of Nigeria, there were no Congolese students at Belgian universities. The Congo was so devoid of political activity in this period that it was known as "Belgium's silent empire".

THE WHITE SETTLERS

In the settler colonies white farmers felt that the contribution they had made to the war effort entitled them to an increased share in the government of their territory, and they intended

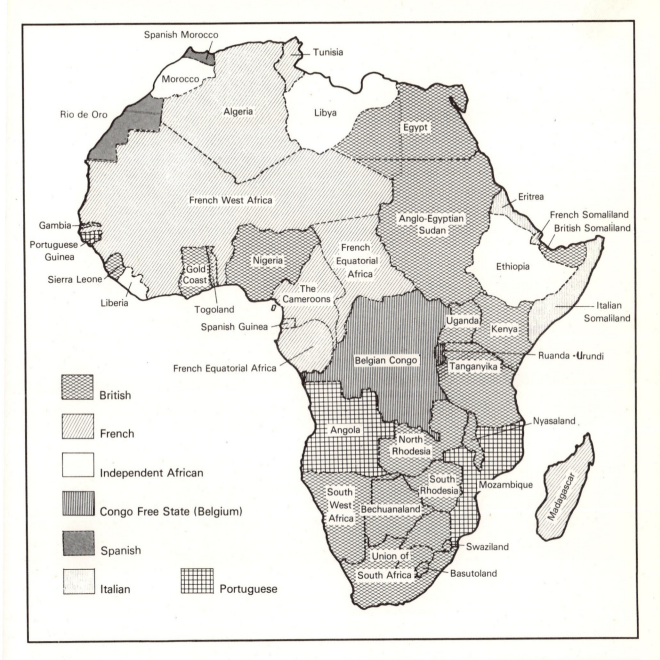

18 The redistribution of colonies after the First World War.

to use this increased power to ensure their position of economic and social supremacy. This trend was heightened by the depression that started in the United States with the Wall Street Crash in 1929. Low prices for agricultural products made white farmers fear for their prosperity. Whether the colonial government resisted or succumbed to pressure from the white farmers was to have a profound effect on the future of the territory in question.

THE EFFECTS OF THE DEPRESSION ON AFRICA

The depressed state of the European economies during this period meant that often the intention to attend more than before to African welfare in practice bore little fruit. In 1929 Great Britain allocated a paltry £1,000,000 per year to African development. Moreover, the steep drop in world prices for commodities such

29

19 An elementary school in Togoland. Such schools were to provide many of the future leaders of Africa.

as cocoa, cotton and ground-nut oil adversely affected the African economies which were dependent on the export of one or two of these major products. The total value of trade of the four British West African colonies fell from £56,000,000 in 1929 to £26,000,000 in 1931. Independent cash-crop farmers were impoverished and Africans in settler colonies suffered as the white populations acquired more political power.

Spontaneous outbursts of protest occurred in many areas. In 1937 Gold Coast cocoa-growers organized a "hold-up", and refused to sell their produce until the price was raised. Such

incidents, however, posed little real threat to the stability of colonial rule.

THE FIRST NATIONALISTS

The important political developments were proceeding silently in the education system, and the results were not be become apparent until the 1940s and '50s. The emergence of a generation of nationalist politicians was primarily a feature of the British colonies, where indirect rule restricted the opportunities open to educated Africans. French Africans found more opportunities in French politics and were consequently

20 **The Ethiopian cavalry leaving Addis Ababa to defend their country against the Italians in 1935.**

less vociferous. (In 1917 Diagne became Under-Secretary for the Colonies in Paris.)

Nationalist politicians, however, were few in number and based almost entirely in the towns. Before they could put effective pressure on colonial governments, they would first have to win the allegiance of the mass of conservative rural Africans and overcome tribal disunity. This process was aided by the drift of impoverished rural Africans to the cities, where shanty-town conditions and unemployment provided an eager audience for nationalist politicians. But, although they had made some progress in Nigeria, the Gold Coast and Kenya by 1939, the bulk of broadly based nationalist movements were not to become effective until the second half of the twentieth century.

Nationalism was most advanced in the Muslim north, where a common religion and culture could unite peoples of vastly different levels of educational and economic attainment, and an educated leadership had existed before the Europeans arrived. Muslim nationalists faced a choice, whether to maintain western standards of economic progress and democracy after

independence or retain a traditional Islamic form of government.

THE ITALIAN INVASION OF ETHIOPIA

Italy was the exception in the general pattern of European rule between the wars. Mussolini's fascist regime wanted to create a vast Italian empire in north and east Africa, which would be totally devoted to supplying Italy's economic needs and absorbing her surplus population. No expense would be spared to make this dream of Italian glory come true.

In May 1936, after a six-month war against Ethiopia in which all the latest technological inventions including poison gas and aerial bombing of civilians had been used against a relatively primitive population, Italy captured

31

Addis Ababa, Emperor Haile Selassie fled into exile and King Victor Emmanuel was declared Emperor of Abyssinia (the Italian name for Ethiopia). The failure of Britain and France to oppose the invasion aroused a distrust among Africans in the good faith of the Europeans. Nkrumah, a student in London at the time, recalled later: "At that time it was as if the whole of London had declared war on me personally." In the longer term, the dignity of Haile Selassie's appeal before the League of Nations in June 1936 was to contribute to the post-1945 climate of opinion in Europe, when black Africans came to be regarded less as children or savages, but as intelligent people capable of running their own affairs.

ALGERIA 1919 - 39

The number of white settlers in Algeria rose to one million by 1939. Frightened by the doubling of the Algerian Muslim population between 1880 and 1930 and by the effects of the depression on farmers, the colons resisted all attempts by the Paris government to give Muslims a greater share in political life. It is

likely that, at this stage, Muslim moderates such as Ferhat Abbas would have been content to live under a just French rule. However, in 1936, when the liberal Governor-General, Maurice Violette, proposed a change in the law that would allow Muslims to become French citizens without sacrificing their religion, colon opposition was so strong that Violette predicted that their intransigence would create an Algerian nationalism where none yet existed:

> These Muslims, when they protest, you become indignant; when they approve, you become suspicious; when they keep quiet, you become afraid . . . these men have no political country of their own . . . . They crave to be admitted to your country. Should you refuse, you may well fear that they will soon create one.

MOROCCO AND TUNISIA

In 1925 a revolt in Spanish Morocco spread to the neighbouring French colony. It was led by a Rif (see page 19), Abd el Krim, who declared a "Rif Republic", complete with a parliament of twenty elected members. This revolt, which was

21 **Typical Rif soldiers.**

crushed by 1926, led to the resignation of Lyautey, the French Resident, in protest at the Paris government's delay in sending reinforcements. Although the Rif Republic borrowed modern political forms and caught the imagination of the Muslim world and of sympathetic Europeans, Abd el Krim's was not a modern nationalist movement. He planned a return to traditional Berber society, with himself as sultan and founder of a new dynasty.

Lyautey's successors in the post of Resident discontinued his tolerant policy towards Muslim customs and institutions. Nationalism emerged in Morocco with the promulgation by the French colonial government in 1930 of the Berber Dahir (Law), which abolished Muslim courts and law and the sultan's right, as a descendant of the prophet Mohammed, to issue laws. By 1934 the Istiqlal or Party of Independence had united the coastal Arabs and nomadic Berbers under the leadership of Sultan Sidi Mohammed.

In Tunisia, likewise, French contempt for Muslim traditions had by 1940 united all sections of society behind the Neo-Destour Party, founded in 1934 by Habib Bourguiba. Although this party drew its strength from Islamic solidarity, Bourguiba's vision of a modern Tunisia embraced equal opportunities for all, regardless of race or religion:

> The Tunisia that we mean to liberate will not be a Tunisia for Muslim, for Jew or for Christian. It will be a Tunisia for all those, without distinction of religion or race, who wish to have it as their country and live under the protection of just laws.

French attempts to crush Istiqlal and Neo-Destour only strengthened their popularity. The arrest of Bourguiba in 1934 led to a ten-fold increase in party membership in three months.

LIBYA

In Libya the Sanussi, under Sayyid Idris, continued their guerilla warfare against Italian rule until they were defeated in 1932. Even though 90 per cent of Libya was desert and the majority of the population were confined to the coastal 3 per cent, Libya was regarded as a valuable extension of Italy's economic potential.

In 1939 it was declared the 19th Region of Italy, and 100,000 Italian peasants had settled there by 1940. Uncultivated land was expropriated for white settlement, thus excluding the nomadic Bedouin from many of their traditional grazing lands. Educated Muslims were eligible for Italian citizenship without surrendering their religion, but the racism of Mussolini's fascist regime ensured that, in practice, Libyans remained second-class citizens.

No nationalist movement emerged, but the Libyans did not simply accept Italian rule. The Bedouin dismissed attempts to resettle them in government villages as "throwing dust in our eyes" and refused to adjust their lifestyle to Italian land laws. With the weakening of Italian authority in the Second World War, the nomads' herds grazed once again with impunity in the colonists' fields.

EGYPT

Fearing that there would be sympathy among Egyptians for the cause of Muslim Turkey during the First World War, Britain annexed Egypt outright in 1914 and sent Khedive Abbas Hilmi into exile. This action, the conscription of Egyptians into the British army in Syria and the requisitioning of camels at low prices for the war effort in Syria brought the support of the urban workers and the peasants (Fellahin) to the Egyptian nationalist movement. By 1919 a mass movement existed in Egypt, which, under the leadership of Zaghul Pasha, was named the Wafd Party.

On 9 March 1919 students in Cairo demonstrated against the British refusal to allow an Egyptian delegation at the Versailles Peace Conference. Civil servants, lawyers, teachers and railway workers came out on strike, and over 1,000 Egyptians died in British attempts to quell the agitation.

In 1922 and 1936 Britain gave Egypt progressive degrees of independence, while maintaining the right to protect British interests by stationing troops in the Canal Zone. King Fuad and his successor, Farouk, accepted the conditions, but the Wafd rejected them, on the grounds that the provisions so shackled Egypt as to make a farce of independence. The Wafd transferred their hostility from the British to the pro-British "puppet king".

BRITISH WEST AFRICA

The effects of British education policies described on page 28 can be seen most graphically in the four West African territories. An educated elite in coastal towns such as Accra (Gold Coast) and Lagos (Nigeria) were frustrated by the lack of political opportunities in rural areas. Although legislative councils were set up to advise the Governors of Nigeria (1922), Sierra Leone (1924) and the Gold Coast (1925), only in a few large towns were the members elected by Africans themselves. In 1928 a Lagos newspaper complained:

> The faint echoes of the protesting voices of elected members have more often than not been drowned in the tumultuous uproar of official "Noes".

Political parties were formed in the towns. The National Congress of British West Africa was founded in 1920 by J. Casely-Hayford, a Gold Coast lawyer, and in 1922 H. Macauley formed the Nigerian National Democratic Party. Neither of these parties succeeded in winning rural support, harnessing the economic grievances of the depression years, or overcoming tribal divisions. Macauley was hampered not only by conservative northern Nigeria, but by the emergence of Ibo nationalism, which demanded an autonomous Ibo state in the east of the country. In 1934 the Lagos Ibo Union was founded, which even had its own national anthem.

In 1935, however, an Ibo, Nmandi Azikiwe, returned to Nigeria from university in the United States and launched a new newspaper, the *West African Pilot*. Whereas previous papers had only had a limited circulation, the *Pilot* set out to win support in rural areas. Azikiwe established cheap dailies in the inland towns of Ibadan and Kano (the capital of Muslim Hausaland). Elsewhere, such a multi-tribal movement had to await the end of the Second World War.

FRENCH WEST AFRICA

Because educated French Africans were given responsible posts in the administration, no significant nationalist movement emerged in either West or Equatorial Africa before 1945. Assimilated West Africans, especially the Senegalese, remained loyal to France and political activity was voluntarily restrained. The first African newspaper outside Senegal appeared in the Ivory Coast only in 1935. All political rights continued to be denied to subjects.

Little progress was made in the promotion of African welfare. When the thirty-year concessions expired in Equatorial Africa, they were not renewed, but they left behind four almost totally undeveloped colonies. When the French novelist, André Gide, visited Equatorial Africa in 1925-26, he wrote:

> We work in a tunnel without any general plan, clear idea or funds . . . . We have only one real port, poor roads, and a poor railroad. French Black Africa does not simply slumber, it snores.

BELGIAN CONGO

The only important developments in the Congo between the wars were the increasing productivity of the Katanga copper mines and the growth of an African urban population in such centres as Leopoldville, the capital, and Elisabethville, the capital of Katanga.

RHODESIA AND NYASALAND

When British South Africa Company rule expired in 1923, the British government surrendered to pressure from the settlers and gave self-governing dominion status to the southern part of Rhodesia. This now enjoyed the same amount of independence as Canada or Australia, with authority over the army and the police force. Southern Rhodesia was henceforth ruled in the interests of the white settlers. In 1930 and 1936 Land Apportionment Acts were passed, in which the best land was reserved for whites. Pass Laws were tightened. African education was neglected. A Rhodesian MP expressed white attitudes:

> The native will continue to be honest if you

leave him with his beads and blankets . . . . If we could clear out every mission station in this country and stop all this fostering of higher native education, we would much sooner become an asset to the Empire.

Northern Rhodesia, on the other hand, received protectorate status in 1923. The discovery in the 1930s of rich copper deposits led to a rise in the white population from 4,000 in 1923 to 57,000 in 1951 and to the emergence of a colour-bar by which blacks were excluded from employment. But all settler demands for comparable dominion status with Southern Rhodesia were resisted. In 1930 Colonial Secretary, Lord Passfield, issued a white paper confirming the paramountcy of African interests over white.

Nationalism continued to develop in protected Nyasaland. In 1943 a Nyasa, J. F. Sangala, appealed for a unified African political movement:

The time is ripe for the Africans of this country to strive for unity so as to obtain the greater development of the peoples and country of Nyasaland.

22 The electrolytic room in the smelter of an Anglo-American copper mine in Northern Rhodesia in the 1950s.

KENYA, UGANDA AND TANGANYIKA

Few developments of note occurred in Uganda and Tanganyika. Events in Kenya might have been expected to follow a similar course to those in Southern Rhodesia. White settlement intensified after the First World War when demobilized officers were encouraged to settle in the White Highlands. Missionary pressure, however, persuaded Colonial Secretary, Lord Devonshire, to declare a protectorate in 1923.

His Majesty's government think it necessary definitely to record their considered opinion that the interests of the African natives must be paramount; and if and when those interests and the interests of the immigrant races should conflict, the former should prevail.

35

This decision was significant for the future. For the next thirty years, however, European society in Kenya maintained its exclusive social supremacy which rejected even poor whites. Insolvent whites were arrested and put on board the next ship for Bombay; there they were abandoned on the quay-side. Confiscation of Kikuyu lands and the exploitation of Kikuyu labour continued. The 1926 Labour Party Report on East Africa concluded:

> The whole organization and administration of government is directed . . . towards compelling the African inhabitants to work for European masters . . . . Every possible device including actual conscription is used to force the native into the labour market. All land, except what has already been sold to Europeans, belongs to the Crown . . . . Africans have only been allowed to occupy certain limited areas on terms of extreme insecurity.

Nationalism developed in Kenya along tribal lines. In 1922 a Kikuyu government clerk, Harry Thuku, founded the Kikuyu National Association and was gaoled. In 1929 the Kikuyu Political Union was formed. If Kenyan nationalism were seriously to challenge British rule, however, it would have to find a way of expanding its appeal to other major tribes such as the Luo. The one man with the genius to unify all the Kenyan tribes was a young Kikuyu, Jomo Kenyatta. For most of the 1930s he was a student in Britain, where he wrote an anthropological thesis on the Kikuyu people: "Facing Mount Kenya". He was not to return home until 1945.

SOUTH WEST AFRICA

The protection of black interests normally bestowed by mandatory status did not extend to South West Africa, mandated to the Union of South Africa. The South African government actively encouraged white settlement, so that by 1935 nearly one third of the land was owned by 32,000 Afrikaner and German farmers. In 1925 the Herero were forcibly evicted from the few lands still remaining to them. When they protested, their houses were burnt and bombs were dropped nearby to frighten them away. The custom of using the native population as a reservoir of cheap labour continued.

UNION OF SOUTH AFRICA

By 1939 the Union of South Africa was by far the wealthiest state in Africa. The price of gold remained unaffected by the slump in world prices. The average income per head of population in South Africa was £22 per annum, while in Tanganyika it was £1.50. Such statistics, however, hide the gross political and economic inequalities there were between black and white South Africans (see page 26). Hertzog of the Afrikaner Nationalist Party explained the situation:

> The European is severe and hard on the native because he is afraid of him. It is the old instinct of self-preservation. And the immediate outcome of this is that so little has been done in the direction of helping the native to advance.

As the Afrikaner Nationalist Party became more influential, it persuaded Smuts' South Africa Party government to pass ever-more repressive legislation against the blacks. In 1932 the Native Service Contract Act made it a criminal offence for an African labourer or his dependants to absent themselves without permission from the property of his employer. The 1927 Immorality Act made mixed marriages illegal. The 1936 Native Representation Act abolished the enfranchisement of educated Cape Africans.

The drift to the towns continued. By 1936 72 per cent of black South Africans lived in areas adjacent to the major cities, where their wages were approximately one eighth of those paid to white workers and where the colour-bar excluded them from skilled work.

Effective African protest was stifled by the landless Africans' absolute dependence on wage-employment for their livelihood, and by the ease with which blackleg labour could be recruited in Mozambique or Basutoland. Prolonged strikes were therefore impossible, as Clemens Kadalie discovered. He was a migrant Nyasa labourer who tried to form the first mass black South African trade union, the Industrial and Commercial Union. In 1930 it staged a dock strike in East London, Cape Province, which lasted only two weeks and was broken by the shipping companies importing casual labour. By 1935 the African National Congress, the opposition movement founded in 1912, still had fewer than 4,000 members.

YOUNG HISTORIAN

A

1 Why and in what ways was the European attitude towards Africans altered by (a) the mandate system, (b) the economic depression, (c) the Italian invasion of Ethiopia?

2 What were the differences in colonial education policy between Britain, France and Belgium? What effects did these differences have on the future development of the colonies of these countries?

3 What conditions were necessary for successful nationalist agitation? To what extent were these conditions present in Africa before 1945? Illustrate your answer with specific examples.

4 Write a paragraph on (a) two protest movements of the 1914-39 period which cannot be termed "nationalist movements", and (b) two nationalist movements of a modern type.

5 What was exceptional about Italian colonial policy in the 1914-1939 period?

6 What events of the 1920s help to account for the different future developments of Southern Rhodesia, Northern Rhodesia and Kenya?

7 What early difficulties hampered the emergence of Kenyan nationalism?

8 Why did no effective African opposition arise in South Africa?

B

1 Write the letter which might have been sent by Lord Lugard, explaining the principles of his colonial policy.

2 Compose the speech which might have been given by a Belgian minister, explaining the reasons behind his country's colonial policy.

3 Write the newspaper article which might have been written by Lyautey, criticizing French policy towards Morocco after his retirement.

4 Compose a letter from a supporter of Azikiwe to a friend, explaining his leader's aims in Nigeria.

5 Compose the letter which a missionary might have sent to Lord Devonshire before his 1923 policy declaration on Kenya.

C

Write the speeches which might have been made by:

1 Haile Selassie before the League of Nations 1936.

2 A supporter of the political rights of Algerian Muslims before the French Assembly.

3 Mussolini on his plans for the future of Libya.

4 A Wafd politician in the Egyptian parliament 1936.

5 A white Kenyan MP on the Devonshire Declaration.

6 An Afrikaner nationalist MP on the need for the 1936 Native Representation Act.

D

Design posters for:

1 Kadalie's Industrial and Commercial Union.

2 The South African government, encouraging settlement in South West Africa.

3 The *West African Pilot*.

THE IMPACT OF THE SECOND WORLD WAR

23 Men of the Nigerian Marine Department. Fourteen thousand Nigerians served in the British army abroad in the Second World War.

THE WAR IN AFRICA

Part of the Second World War was waged on African soil. In 1940 the Italians tried unsuccessfully to wrest Egypt and the Suez Canal, gateways to the Middle East oilfields, from British control. The defeat suffered by the Italian army at the hands of British troops under Wavell led to the expulsion of Italy from Ethiopia, Eritrea and Somaliland. With the Suez Canal again as the goal, the German General Rommel and his Afrika Korps took up the struggle against the British in North Africa until his final defeat in the spring of 1943. As a result of the so-called "desert war", Haile Selassie was reinstated in Addis Ababa, Eritrea was ceded to Ethiopia as compensation, Somaliland was placed under the United Nations Trusteeship Council (which replaced the Mandates Commission), and large areas of Tunisia and Libya were devastated.

After the fall of France in June 1940, French colonies were caught up in the struggle between de Gaulle's Free French and the German-sponsored Vichy government. All French colonial governors, with the exception of the Guyanan Governor of Equatorial Africa, Felix Eboué, supported Vichy until 1943. Eboué was accused of treason by a fellow governor: "You have, by a deliberate and plotted act, broken the cohesion of the Empire."

In South Africa future Prime Ministers Verwoerd and Vorster openly supported the Nazi cause as a gesture of defiance against the British, whom they regarded as an alien colonial power.

AFRICAN CONTRIBUTIONS TO THE WAR EFFORT

African soldiers from British and French colonies did active service in Ethiopia, North

Africa and Burma. Settler colonies, however, were careful to include as few Africans as possible in their contributions to the Allied armies. So, whereas 14,000 Nigerians served in the British army abroad, Southern Rhodesia recruited only 1,505, and none of these were involved in the use of firearms.

With the Japanese conquest of South-East Asia in 1941 and 1942, supplies of rubber and minerals such as tin became scarce, and African economies were mobilized to compensate for the shortages. In Senegal the "Battle of the Groundnuts" was launched to increase supplies of oil. Governor Boisson declared in 1943:

> We must produce. The next groundnut crop in Senegal must in particular be a great success . . . . I conclude with an equation: Work=Victory=Liberation of the Motherland.

THE EFFECTS OF THE WAR ON AFRICAN ECONOMIC AND SOCIAL LIFE

In spite of the hardships of forced labour and conscription, colonial economies flourished during the war. Some colonies became self-sufficient for the first time. Because raw materials could not be so easily shipped to Europe for processing, local industries were boosted and this, in turn, hastened the process of urbanization. Many African towns doubled in size during the war.

Africans who had experienced life abroad imported new ideas. A British Commission reported in 1946:

> In the Second World War in particular he [the African] was brought into contact with the outside world, and he established a new relationship with men of other races. He returned to civilian life with changed tastes and standards, but soon found that the opportunities for earning a level of income which he had lived up to in the army did not exist.

THE NATIONALISTS

Future nationalist leaders, Nkrumah (Gold Coast), Kenyatta (Kenya), Senghor (Senegal) and Houphouet-Boigny (Ivory Coast), spent the war years in London or the United States and their sense of national consciousness was strengthened. Nkrumah recalled:

> The political conscience of African students was aroused, and whenever they met they talked of little else but nationalist politics and colonial liberation movements.

A great impact was made by the Atlantic Charter, agreed between Britain and the USA in 1941, with its affirmation of the right of national self-determination, and by the Afro-Asian non-aligned conference held at Bandung in Indonesia in 1955, with its sweeping condemnation of colonialism. An Indonesian nationalist remarked:

> Before Bandung, many had struggled alone, unaided and often unnoticed, fighting first for independence and then for survival. Now it was clear that these hitherto disregarded peoples were no longer alone.

Once the Gold Coast had attained independence in 1957 (see page 46), it acted as an inspiration to nationalist movements elsewhere in Africa, a process that Nkrumah actively encouraged:

> Freedom for the Gold Coast will be a fountain of inspiration from which other African colonial territories can draw when the time comes. Independence for the Gold Coast is meaningless unless it is linked up with the total liberation of the continent.

NATIONALISM AND THE MASSES

The mass support for nationalism which had been lacking before 1939 was provided by the events of the war years. The humiliations suffered by France in Europe and by Britain in the Far East, and the numerous close contacts made between ordinary European and African soldiers destroyed for ever the myth of white invincibility. In August 1949 a *Times* editorial drew this conclusion from the fact that so many British troops had passed through West Africa since 1939:

In such a large army there have been sufficient cases of human frailty, of one sort or another, for the alert African to realize that here was a creature with his own limitations.

Moreover, African ex-soldiers were no longer content with African living standards. Increased literacy had led to an increased awareness of the contemporary international opinions embodied in the Atlantic and Bandung Charters. A Nigerian soldier wrote in 1945:

We have been told what we fought for. That is "freedom". We want freedom, nothing but freedom.

Trade unionism developed, as urbanization and industrialization expanded. In 1947 a general strike took place in Tanganyika, and French West African railwaymen stopped work for 160 days.

In order to galvanize these discontents in the interests of the independence movements, nationalist politicians concentrated on persuading Africans that a better standard of living

24   The beginning of work on the Kariba Dam on the border between Northern and Southern Rhodesia. At flood stage the river reaches the level of the road.

would automatically result from the departure of the colonial masters. "Seek ye first the political kingdom" became the slogan of Kwame Nkrumah.

CHANGES IN EUROPEAN ATTITUDES

German war-time propaganda, aimed at fermenting rebellion in British and French colonies, and the struggle between the Free French and the Vichy regime for the allegiance of the French territories, both made it necessary for colonial governments, for the first time, to earn rather than assume the loyalty of their coloured subjects. In 1944, at Brazzaville, the capital of French Equatorial Africa, de Gaulle promised vast increases in French financial aid for the promotion of African health and welfare.

This was to be French Africa's reward for providing France in 1940 with "her refuge and the starting point for her liberation".

The changed atmosphere found expression in an increased concern for African welfare and an abandonment of the doctrine of self-sufficiency for the colonies. Britain passed a Colonial Development Act in 1945, which by 1955 had pumped £210 million into African economies. Work began on ambitious projects such as the hydro-electric power station in Jinja in Uganda and the Kariba Dam on the border between Northern and Southern Rhodesia. De Gaulle organized a conference of colonial governors at Brazzaville in 1944, at which he stressed French obligations to assist the economic development and social welfare of her subjects. The Indigenat was abolished, health services were improved and educational standards raised. In British colonies, likewise, educational provision was vastly increased. Four university colleges (attached to the University of London) were set up at Ibadan in Nigeria, Makerere in Uganda, Achimota in the Gold Coast and Khartoum in the Sudan. By 1958 1 in 3 of all Nigerian children of school age (5-12 years) were attending some form of educational institution.

In 1945 the British and French governments thought of self-government for Africa only in terms of progress towards a limited degree of local autonomy within the British Empire or French Community. According to Labour MP, Herbert Morrison, to give independence to Africa would be like "giving a child of ten a latch key, a bank account and a shot gun". Democratic government was introduced at local level. In British colonies indirect rule by chiefs was replaced by rule by elected local councils. France introduced the pattern of elected communes used in mainland France. The post-

25 The university of Makerere in Uganda was set up after the Second World War. The International Atomic Energy Agency sponsored a programme at the university to study the use of insecticides in controlling the tse-tse fly.

war Gold Coast constitution established a legislative council on which elected Africans outnumbered those chosen by the Governor, and the intention was announced "to appoint Africans to senior appointments wherever suitable Africans could be found".

In 1957 the Gold Coast achieved independence. But the radical conversion of the British and French governments to a support of full independence occurred relatively suddenly in the very late 1950s. In 1958 de Gaulle offered the French colonies the choice between self-government as independent republics within the French Community and complete independence and the severing of all ties with France. British Prime Minister, Harold Macmillan, and Colonial Secretary, Iain Macleod, were so impressed by the force of African agitation that they formulated a new policy. In his memoirs Macmillan recalls the impact made on him by these words of a colonial governor:

> If . . . 15 or 20 years were to be applied to learning the job, increasing their experience of local government . . . . why then I would be all for it. But this is not what will happen. All the most intelligent men capable of government will be in rebellion. I will have to put them in prison. There they will learn nothing about administration; only about hatred and revenge. They will not be fruitful but wasted years; so I say, give them independence now.

In 1960 British policy became public knowledge in a speech which Macmillan, on the first-

26 A new constitution for Nigeria after the Second World War gave more places on the Legislative Council to elected African members than to British government officials. The first Legislative Council of this arrangement listens to the Governor's speech, 1947.

ever tour of English-speaking Africa by a serving British Prime Minister, made before the South African parliament;

> The most striking of all the impressions I have formed since I left London a month ago is of the strength of this African consciousness. The wind of change is blowing through this continent, and whether we like it or not this growth of national consciousness is a political fact, and our national policies must take account of it.

The transition to independence in most British and French colonies was smooth and relatively peaceful. Independent African governments were left with constitutions based on government by a democratically elected parliament — the system of "majority rule". Settler colonies, however, were usually unwilling to accept this system, which would inevitably result in a black African government. The extent to which majority rule could be imposed on a

27   Cameroon children parade as part of their celebrations of independence.

colony by the home government depended on the extent to which the white community already held sufficient political and military power to allow them to be obstructive. In some areas Britain sought to avoid the issue by introducing "multi-racial" constitutions, in which each racial group, regardless of size, was equally represented in the government. African nationalists fought fervently against such a dilution of the majority rule principle.

Belgium and Portugal did not share in this conversion. In 1960 President Salazar of Portugal praised the spiritualism of the Portuguese way of life, which prevented Portugal from capitulating to materialist doctrines or the "artificial sentiment" of the African right to independence. Belgium continued to exclude the Congolese from responsible positions until 1960. In that year the police force, the Force Publique, possessed not a single African officer.

YOUNG HISTORIAN

A

1 In what ways and why was the status of Europeans in Africa diminished during the Second World War?
2 In what ways did African economies benefit from the war?
3 What new political influences entered Africa during the Second World War?
4 Why did nationalism develop so rapidly as a mass movement after 1939?
5 Why did Britain and France convert so suddenly to an acceptance of African independence?
6 Give examples of the ways in which independence might be delayed.

B

Write the letters which might have been sent by:
1 A French African in 1940, describing his confusion about where his allegiance should lie.
2 An African soldier, returning to his native village in 1946.
3 An educated African in a settler colony, on the occasion of the independence of Ghana, describing his hopes and fears for the future of *his* country.
4 A British colonial governor 1959, urging swift evolution of his colony towards independence.
5 The governor of a settler colony, opposing the above for his territory.

C

1 Write an appeal that might have been issued by the British army advancing in Ethiopia in 1940, urging the local inhabitants to aid them against the Italians.
2 Write a manifesto that might have been written by a nationalist politician in a colonial state in 1958 (you may choose the state), urging his countrymen to follow the example of Ghana.
3 Write a leaflet to be disseminated by German agents in Algeria in 1939, urging Muslims to overthrow the French colonial government.

D

Design posters that might have been issued by colonial governments advertizing the following:
(a) The groundnut campaign in Senegal
(b) The opening of the Kariba Dam
(c) The University College at Ibadan.

FROM 1945 TO INDEPENDENCE IN THE NORTH AND WEST

EGYPT TO 1956

Between 1936 and 1950 the Wafd Party won a large majority at every election to the Egyptian Parliament; the king, however, with the support of sections of the army, attempted to rule as an autocrat, ignoring Parliament as much as possible. Although Farouk and the Wafd politicians remained bitter enemies, the once revolutionary party became, in this period, as corrupt and out-of-touch with the people of Egypt as the despised King or the British administration before him. In Cairo by 1952 over 100,000 males were officially registered as unemployed. In elections, the majority of votes were bought and sold by a handful of wealthy landowners and merchants. Farouk's regime had been humiliated in 1949, when the newly created state of Israel defeated the combined armies of the Arab League. In a desperate attempt to buy popularity, Farouk declared the 1936 treaty with Britain null and void in 1951.

In 1952 a coup instigated by young army officers drove the king into exile. General Neguib became president, but the real power behind the movement was thirty-four-year-old Colonel Gamal Abdul Nasser, who ousted Neguib in 1954.

Nasser's aims were threefold: to end foreign influence in Egypt; to create social justice; and to make Egypt the leader of the liberation movements in Africa and the Arab world. He accomplished the first aim when he nationalized the Anglo-French-owned Suez Canal in 1956 and successfully defended Egypt against ill-advised British and French military retaliation — in the so-called Suez Crisis. After seventy-five years Britain finally renounced her right to intervene in Egypt.

ALGERIA UNTIL 1962

After 1945, Violette's prediction about Algerian nationalism came true (see page 32). France's loss of prestige in 1940 and the stationing of anti-colonial American troops in Algeria between 1943 and 1945 were compounded by the racial riots at Setif in 1945, in which over one hundred Europeans and thousands of Muslims were killed. In 1947 half a dozen young nationalists, led by Ahmed Ben Bella, founded the Organisation Secrète, a tiny guerilla army of independence. In 1954 the Organisation, now renamed the Front de Libération National (FLN), began a war against the French that lasted until 1962. The duration and the ferocity of the war can be traced to two factors. The brutality of French police methods, which included torture and the mass arrest of entire villages and streets on mere suspicion, drove the majority of Muslims on to the side of the FLN. And yet the Paris government was prevented from peacefully accepting the principle of Algerian independence by resistance from French colons and French paratroop regiments stationed in Algeria. Prime Minister Guy Mollet, suspected of being favourable towards Algerian independence, was pelted with cabbages and tomatoes on a visit to Algiers in 1957. He swiftly reversed his policy.

In 1958 the French army brought General de Gaulle to power. They hoped that he would quash all talk of an independent Algeria. De Gaulle, however, realized the futility of wasting

28 In 1952 Neguib (second from right) led an army coup against King Farouk of Egypt. But in his turn, Neguib was ousted in 1954 by Nasser (seated at the table on Neguib's right).

lives and money fighting against what was probably inevitable anyway. In September 1959 he made a nationwide speech on radio and television:

> I deem it necessary that recourse to self-determination be here and now proclaimed. In the name of France and the Republic . . . I pledge myself to ask the Algerians . . . what, when all is said and done, they wish to be; and, on the other hand, all Frenchmen, to endorse that choice.

Between 1959 and 1962 colons and army tried to bully de Gaulle away from this policy, as they had bullied Mollet before him. Dissident army officers such as Massu and Salan formed the OAS (Organisation de l'Armée Secrète — secret army), which pursued a campaign of terrorism, against Gaullists in Algeria and France, including attempts to assassinate de Gaulle himself. However, on 2 July 1962 Algeria became independent under the presidency of Ben Bella.

TUNISIA AND MOROCCO

In 1956 France peacefully granted independence to Tunisia and Morocco under President Bourguiba and Sultan Mohammed V respectively. There were fewer French colonists than in Algeria (250,000 in Tunisia and 300,000 in Morocco) and French emotional attachment was much less. A sizeable proportion of the European population remained after independence.

THE GOLD COAST

Independence came first to Muslim North Africa; the pace in tropical Africa was set by the Gold Coast. Unusually wealthy, and with few serious tribal rivalries, the Gold Coast produced in 1947 a charismatic leader who realized the necessity of converting the nationalism of the educated few into a mass movement. In 1949 Nkrumah founded the Convention Peoples Party (CPP). It evolved the popular slogan "self-government

29 The OAS in Algeria planted bombs in Muslim shops and cafés as part of their campaign of terrorism against giving Algeria independence.

30 On 29 June 1962, four days before the independence of Algeria, FLN troops, who had been fighting for independence since 1954, raise their flag at a village near Algiers.

31 Muslims celebrate independence in Algiers.

now" and strove to persuade all discontented groups that independence alone was the answer to their social and economic problems. He utilized the 1948 ex-servicemen's demonstrations to spark off a wave of anti-British demonstrations throughout the country. He embarked on country-wide tours and in 1950 declared "Positive Action" — a civil disobedience campaign consisting of "strikes, boycotts and non-cooperation based on the principles of absolute non-violence". Although he was imprisoned in 1950, the widespread support for Nkrumah convinced Governor Arden-Clarke that independence was inevitable. He devoted his efforts to persuading the British government to cooperate with Nkrumah to ensure a steady and peaceful transfer of power. In 1957 the Gold Coast became the independent state of Ghana. Perhaps here can be seen most clearly the crucial role played by the colonial government in deciding whether the transition would be violent or peaceful. In his autobiography, *Ghana*, Nkrumah gave this account of the independence celebrations:

> "Prime Minister", the Governor said, as he extended his hand to me, "this is a great day for you. It is the end of what you have struggled for." "It is the end of what we have been struggling for, Sir Charles", I corrected him. "You have contributed a great deal towards this; in fact I might not have succeeded without your help and co-operation. This is a very happy day for us both".

NIGERIA

Given the changing attitudes in Britain, Azikiwe's mass movement in Nigeria (see page 34) had little difficulty in committing the British government to independence in principle. However, achievement was delayed until 1960 by tribal rivalries. The Muslim north, being the most populous of the three tribal regions, would dominate any parliament chosen by direct elections and this aroused deep fears among the Yoruba and Ibo. On the other hand, the emirs, the Muslim chiefs, feared that the sophisticated, westernized southerners would control the administration. The north therefore resisted independence as part of a unified Nigeria and

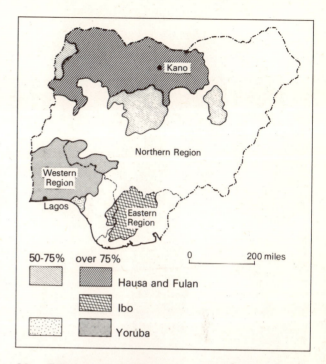

32 Tribal groups in Nigeria.

even agitated for secession. In 1953 there were anti-southern riots in Kano, which resulted in 36 deaths and 240 injuries.

Eventually, after seven years of delay, a federal form of constitution evolved, in which each region was to be allowed to develop at its own pace. The federal Prime Minister, however, was a northerner, Sir Abubakar Tafawa Balewa, and ethnic fears were not assuaged. When visiting newly independent Nigeria in 1960, Macmillan was made acutely aware that no Nigerian nation yet existed:

> These visits to the different regions, although so short, did at least allow me to realize how difficult had been the formation of the Federation with its immense variety of peoples, religions and traditions.

FRENCH WEST AND EQUATORIAL AFRICA

Few African politicians in French West and Equatorial Africa thought in terms of complete independence. They aimed rather at self-government within the French community. In 1957 the Senegalese leader, Leopold Senghor, said:

In Africa, when children grow up, they leave the parents' hut, and build a hut of their own by its side. Believe me, we don't want to leave the French compound. We have grown up in it and it is good to be alive in it. We simply want to build our own huts.

The form that the association with France would take was the subject of a dispute between Houphouet-Boigny of the Ivory Coast, Senghor of Senegal and Sekou Touré of Guinea. In Senghor's opinion, only a federation of all former French colonies would be strong enough to ensure economic prosperity. Houphouet, however, feared that in a federation the wealthy Ivory Coast would have to subsidize her poorer neighbours, and so he favoured independence for all the states as separate republics. The issue was solved by de Gaulle's announcement in 1958 that all French colonies were to be offered the choice between self-government as separate republics within the French community and complete independence severing all ties with France (see page 42). In a referendum in September 1958 all French African colonies

(see page 42)

33 Violence broke out after independence was granted to the Congo and refugees fled to Northern Rhodesia. The cars had been stoned by terrorists.

voted for cooperation with France, except Guinea. Sekou Touré announced: "We prefer poverty in freedom to riches in slavery". France fulfilled her threat; by November 1958 all French aid and technicians had been removed; even the telephones were disconnected and the wine cellars emptied.

THE CONGO TO 1960

"It is true", said the Belgian Information Service in 1959, "that no one votes in the Congo. The Belgians prefer administration to politics." Belgium had denied political experience and higher education to the Congolese, and so, when political parties were first formed in the late 1950s, they were based on tribal loyalties and local issues. They looked back to the kingdoms of the pre-colonial Congo, such as Katanga, rather than forward to a united modern state.

Belgium had justified her policy by claiming that Belgian rule would last indefinitely. In 1959, however, came a dramatic reversal of policy. "We are fearful", said a Belgian government spokesman, "lest another Algeria creates itself in the Congo". In June 1960 a party of Congolese politicians attended a conference in Ostend, at which they expected to be offered a lengthy transitional period to independence. Instead they were given a date for independence less than six months away — 30 June 1960. Lumumba, one of the few Congolese politicians to believe in a united Congo, became Prime Minister and the majority of skilled Belgian personnel fled the country.

ETHIOPIA AND LIBYA

Libya became independent in 1950 under the Sanussi King Idris, not through the agitation of a nationalist movement, but by a decision of the United Nations Trusteeship Council. The rights of the Italian settlers were guaranteed by treaty, but their future obviously depended on the good will of future Libyan governments. The poverty of Libya's economic prospects was transformed by the discovery of large oil reserves in June 1959.

Ethiopia remained under the rule of Haile Selassie throughout the independence era. Her internal history is covered on pages 70-72.

YOUNG HISTORIAN

A

1 Why was the monarchy overthrown in Egypt?
2 Why was the struggle for independence so bitter in Algeria, yet relatively peaceful in Tunisia and Morocco?
3 What were the respective contributions of Sir C. Arden-Clarke and K. Nkrumah to Ghanaian independence?
4 Analyse the ways in which tribal rivalries could be a threat to political stability after independence. Describe the difficulties that arose in *one* West or Central African state.
5 Would you consider that Belgium was primarily responsible for the difficulties experienced by the Congo after 1960?

B

Write a possible dialogue between the following:
1 A colon and a Gaullist in 1960.
2 A Muslim from northern Nigeria and an Ibo in 1958.
3 Houphouet-Boigny and Senghor over the future of French West Africa.

C

1 Write the manifesto which might have been issued by Sekou Touré in 1958, urging his people to vote "no" in the forthcoming referendum.
2 Write the leader article which might have appeared in (a) a British, (b) an Egyptian newspaper at the end of the Suez crisis.
3 Write the leader article which might have appeared in (a) a liberal French, (b) an Algerian newspaper on de Gaulle's 1959 speech promising self-determination to Algeria.
4 Write the speech which might have been made before the Belgian parliament, justifying the change of policy towards the Congo. Compose a critical reply to this speech.

D

Some of the events mentioned in this chapter were of importance not only to Africa but also to world affairs. See if you can discover more about:
1 1956 Suez crisis.
2 De Gaulle's presidency in France.
3 Macmillan's Conservative government 1956-63.

FROM 1945 TO INDEPENDENCE IN THE SOUTH AND EAST

EAST AFRICA — TANGANYIKA, UGANDA AND KENYA

The first Tanganyikan political party was not founded until 1954, when Julius Nyerere formed the Tanganyika African National Union (TANU). In spite of the country's political backwardness, the path to independence was relatively smooth, because of the climate of opinion in Britain in the late 1950s and the protection afforded to Tanganyika by its trusteeship status (see page 28). (Tanganyika had been transferred from the League of Nations to the United Nations in 1945.) The most explosive issue was the fate of the few white settlers. Nyerere resisted any attempt to impose a multi-racial constitution. As early as 1954 he had petitioned the United Nations:

> The Africans of this country would further like to be assured . . . that this territory, though multi-racial in population, is primarily an African country and must be developed as such.

However, once the principle of majority rule had been established, he insisted that the Europeans and Asians who had made Tanganyika their home should be regarded as equal citizens with the Africans:

> There are Africans who say that when Tanganyika achieves independence Europeans and Asians will suffer. These are not the words of TANU. They are the words of fools.

Ugandan independence was delayed until 1962 by Bugandan opposition. Bugandans feared that majority rule would erode their privileged position, and they played in Ugandan politics the role played elsewhere by white settlers. The Kabaka of Buganda ordered his subjects not to participate in the 1961 elections, and an unsuccessful appeal was made to Queen Elizabeth, asking that Buganda be allowed to secede. The final constitution of 1962 permitted the Bugandans to maintain a privileged role. They were to control their own prisons, police, schools and hospitals; the High Court of Buganda was to continue; the Kabaka became Ugandan Head of State, and Kampala remained the capital. The central Ugandan government, however, was led by a non-Bugandan, Dr Milton Obote.

Progress towards majority rule in Kenya was obstructed by settler dissent and tribal animosities. In 1951 Kenyan whites demanded an assurance that:

> African nationalism on the lines of West Africa was not her Majesty's Government's policy for Kenya and that any statements which suggested such a thing was possible should be considered as seditious.

In 1952 members of a Kikuyu secret society, the Mau Mau, attacked European farms and Africans who supported British rule, and provoked an equally brutal retaliation from British troops. The state of emergency lasted until 1960. Kenyatta was arrested as Mau Mau ring leader, but this charge has never been proved.

In spite of the violence, the arrival of Macmillan's friend Macleod at the Colonial Office in 1959 meant that majority rule was eventually accepted for Kenya as elsewhere. "At

34 To celebrate the independence of Tanganyika, a flag-raising party climbed to the top of Mount Kilimanjaro, to hoist Tanganyika's green, black and gold flag.

one blow", commented a white politician, "power was transferred to the Africans". The actual drafting of a constitution for Kenya was made difficult by the existence of two rival tribal-based parties. The Kenyan African National Union (KANU) had an almost exclusively Kikuyu membership; the Kenyan African Peoples Union (KAPU), which drew its support from the smaller tribes, feared Kikuyu domination in a constitution based on majority rule, and demanded a federal constitution giving considerable autonomy to individual tribes. Only the personal magnetism of Kikuyu leader, Kenyatta, enabled independence to be achieved in December 1963, after a landslide KANU election victory. It seemed that the continued existence of a united Kenya depended on one

man's life, and many shared Macmillan's pessimistic prognosis:

> If we have to give independence to Kenya, it may well prove another Congo.

THE RHODESIAS AND NYASALAND TO 1965

In 1953 the British Government supported the creation of a Central African Federation, which united Northern and Southern Rhodesia and Nyasaland under a federal government. As Macmillan recalled, to the British government, such a union made sound economic sense:

> The economic advantages of making a single area of these vast territories were overwhelming and had been generally accepted

53

35   Africans whose village has just been raided by the Mau Mau run for safety to the whites with their firearms.

. . . . Indeed without federation the building of the great Kariba Dam could scarcely have been undertaken, from which Northern Rhodesia was to draw the vital supplies of electric power for the copper belt.

To the Northern and Southern Rhodesian white leaders, Sir Roy Welensky and Sir Geoffrey Huggins, such a move would solidify white supremacy in all three areas.

Politically and economically, Africans in the Federation became second-class citizens. In 1958 a commission on urban African affairs reported:

There is really no room to doubt that from one-fifth to two-fifths of urban Africans in the Rhodesias are not earning enough to keep their families; and of those with two children or more the majority are undernourished and underclothed.

In Nyasaland in particular, among the politically-conscious, the Federation was immensely unpopular. When the Nyasa nationalist leader, Dr Hastings Banda, returned in 1959 after forty years' absence, demonstrations led to the declaration of a state of emergency. Macmillan recalled his visit to Nyasaland in 1960:

The prevailing impression left upon me was that in Nyasaland the cause of federation was almost desperate because of the strength of African opposition against it.

Convinced by African protests, the British government withdrew its support for the Central African Federation and was able swiftly to effect a transition to African majority rule in Northern Rhodesia and Nyasaland. These former protectorates became independent in 1964 as Zambia and Malawi, under the presidency of Kenneth Kaunda and Hastings Banda respectively.

In Southern Rhodesia the hard-line Rhodesia Front, the white supremacist party, won the 1962 election. For three years negotiations took place with Britain for independence under

36   Jomo Kenyatta speaking at Kenya's independence ceremony.

a settler-dominated constitution. British refusal led in November 1965 to a unilateral declaration of independence (UDI) by Rhodesia Front Prime Minister, Ian Smith, who claimed that Rhodesia had thus "struck a blow for the preservation of justice, civilization and Christianity".

Resistance by Africans to UDI was minimal. Effective nationalist opposition in Rhodesia encountered the same obstacles as that in South Africa (see page 36). When UDI was declared, Sithole and Nkomo, the leaders of the Zimbabwe African Peoples Union (ZAPU), had already been imprisoned. The future development of Black Rhodesian nationalism was to fulfil the prophesy made by Nkomo in 1962 that increasing African frustration at the failure of legitimate political activity would lead to the growth of violent movements.

SOUTH AFRICA TO 1961

The aims of white government in South Africa had not changed since the 1930s. The racist Afrikaner Nationalist Party, in power continuously since 1948, looked to the policy of apartheid as the solution to white fears. All Africans were to be repatriated in tribal homelands or "Bantustans". According to an official South African government publication,

> The Republic of South Africa has its own special part to play in human affairs. It bears responsibility for a multi-racial population more complex than any on earth. To meet this situation it has a clear-cut policy based on three considerations:
> That the people of South Africa do not compose one nation but distinctive white and black — or Bantu — nations.
> That throughout Africa today African peoples are claiming the right to express their own personality and nationhood.
> That the white nation in South Africa has the same right.

Complete territorial separation of blacks and whites was impossible, however, as cheap African labour was needed for the white economy. Where the two races were interdependent, blacks and coloureds (half-castes) were subject to many restrictions. They were forced to live in separate communities on the

37   Africans recruited for labour in South Africa.

Apartheid to him was more than a political philosophy, it was a religion; a religion based on the Old Testament rather than the new . . . he was as convinced as John Knox that he alone could be right.

In 1952 an African Defiance campaign was started by Chief Albert Luthuli, who later won the Nobel Peace Prize. The aim of the movement was to defy racial laws by means of peaceful

outskirts of towns, such as the suburbs of Soweto and Sophiatown outside Johannesburg, and commute daily to work. Separate and inferior facilities were provided in everything from park benches to universities. Pass laws restricted the access of Africans to urban areas, and there were strict limitations on the jobs available to Africans. In 1953 the Bantu Education Act placed all African education in government hands and ensured that Africans could be denied any education other than that needed to fit them for menial jobs. In 1950 a Population Register was established to decide on the racial make-up of every South African.

All dissent, whether from black or white, was suppressed by the Suppression of Communism Act. By this act, the Minister of Justice could ban from public affairs anyone whom he suspected, with or without proof, of being a communist. In 1961 the police were granted the power to interrogate a suspect for twelve days without making charges (and this was raised to 90 days in 1962 and 180 days in 1972).

In 1960 Africans peacefully demonstrating against the pass laws at Sharpeville in the Transvaal were shot at by police and 180 were killed. In protest, Commonwealth prime ministers, led by Nyerere of Tanganyika, drove South Africa from the Commonwealth. Macmillan graphically summed up the inflexible dedication of Prime Minister Verwoerd to the doctrine of white supremacy:

assaults on segregated institutions (similar tactics were tried by Martin Luther King and the Civil Rights Movement in the United States). The protesters sat on benches marked "whites only"; buses were boycotted in Alexandra township; and passes were burnt. While limited successes were achieved, such as the prevention of a steep rise in bus fares, any real breakthrough to political equality for Africans was stalled by the strength of the South African police state.

SOUTH WEST AFRICA

South West Africa's incorporation as the fifth state of South Africa continued. When the United Nations declared in 1961 that South Africa was unfit to administer her mandated

38   Separate facilities for blacks and whites in Durban.

territories, the South African government refused to accept the jurisdiction. (Internal developments in South West Africa are dealt with on page 83.)

THE PORTUGUESE COLONIES TO 1961

While other European governments were withdrawing from Africa, Portugal was, for the first time, evolving a coherent policy, which would result in the conversion of Mozambique, Angola and Guinea-Bissau into overseas provinces of Portugal. White settlement was encouraged on a large scale; the status of Indigenas was abolished. Under this system, independence could not evolve by common consent; it would have to be seized by force. (Developments in the Portuguese colonies in the 1960s and '70s are dealt with on page 83.)

YOUNG HISTORIAN

A

1 Why was the path to independence much smoother in Tanganyika than in Kenya and Uganda?
2 Why was the formation of a Central African Federation supported by (a) the British government, (b) white settlers? Why did most Africans oppose the Federation and why was it finally dissolved?
3 Why did the UDI occur in Southern Rhodesia?
4 What is apartheid? Why cannot it be rigidly applied in South Africa?
5 Why has there been so little opposition to apartheid since 1948?

B

Compose the letters which might have been sent by:
1 The Kabaka of Buganda to the British government, opposing independence for a united Uganda.
2 A Mau Mau activist, justifying his activities.
3 A white Kenyan farmer, opposing independence.
4 A black factory-worker living in Soweto, describing his daily life.

C

From this and the two preceding chapters, construct an account of Macmillan's attitude towards colonial independence, giving specific examples of his assessment of the political situation in different areas.

D

Design posters for:
1 TANU
2 Dr Banda's anti-Central African Federation movement.
3 Rhodesia Front party 1965.
4 Luthuli's anti-pass laws campaign.

THE PROBLEMS OF INDEPENDENCE I

In his speech at the Tanganyikan independence celebrations, Nyerere told his audience: "We ourselves can lift from our own shoulders the burdens of poverty, ignorance and disease". Many Africans shared this belief that freedom from colonial rule would automatically solve economic problems, unite rival tribes and provide a permanent link between the few who governed and the mass of the people. Moreover, the new African nations almost universally

39   Civil war in the Congo lasted for four years after independence. These men of the Congolese army are being trained for warfare in the jungle.

inherited a western-style parliamentary democratic system, which western observers optimistically assumed would function as successfully in Africa as in Europe and North America. Most of these hopes were to be shattered in the course of the next twenty years.

MINORITIES AND DIVISIONS

For many Africans, loyalty to their tribe came before loyalty to an artificially created state.

The 1960s witnessed a spate either of secessionist movements or of tribal quarrels over who should control the machinery of government. For example, within months of Congolese independence, Katanga had broken away and four years of civil war followed. In 1977 and

1978 Katanga (now renamed Shaba Province) again tried twice to secede. Similarly, between 1967 and 1970 a tragic civil war raged between Nigeria and the breakaway Ibo state of Biafra. In Uganda, tribal jealousies led to the exile of the Kabaka of Buganda by President Obote, and then to Obote's own deposition by a representative of a rival tribe, Colonel Idi Amin. Civil wars also occurred in the Sudan (Muslim north against pagan and Christian south), in Ethiopia, and in Chad, where the unsuccessful 1979 reconciliation talks were attended by no fewer than nine different ethnic factions. Even tiny French Somaliland (Djibouti) achieved independence, in 1977, in the midst of racial clashes between the Afars and the Issars.

Most African leaders publicly adhere to Nyerere's non-racialism, but have been under strong pressure from their followers to introduce policies of Africanization — that is, replacing European or Asian personnel with native-born Africans. Italians in Libya (1971), non-citizen Asians in Kenya (1968), Asians in Uganda (1972), and the French in Tunisia have been among the groups expelled. Often such people took with them much-needed technical and commercial expertise. Even Nyerere faced an army mutiny in 1964 which forced him to remove British officers and replace them with Africans.

ECONOMIC PROBLEMS

Many African states are desperately poor in resources. The former French West African states of Dahomey (Benin), Guinea, Niger and Upper Volta are among the twenty-five most underdeveloped nations in the world. Moreover, primitive economies are particularly vulnerable to climatic disasters. The 1973-74 drought brought starvation to the Sahel states, while two years of deficient rainfall in normally self-sufficient Tanzania (the new name for Tanganyika) forced Nyerere to pay out £80,000,000 in foreign exchange for food imports.

The colonial legacy brought further disadvantages. For example, in West Africa, each national railway system had been built with a different gauge, and it proved impossible after independence to weld them into one single system.

Even in wealthier states, the colonial governments had developed the cultivation of commodities such as copper or cocoa which

40 One of the problems of independence was the departure of the white population, with their skills. The farms of Afrikaners, who left Kenya, became overgrown and derelict.

61

41   At a time of drought in Ethiopia in 1974, destitute farmers signed on for road building gangs.

would be immediately profitable and neglected the subsistence agriculture on which the majority of the population depended for their livelihood. States such as Senegal, Zambia and Ghana depended on export revenues for the purchase of food, and so faced famine when commodity prices fell. Moreover, the benefits of a cash-crop or mineral-exporting economy fell only to the few who were directly involved. At independence, the copper miners of Katanga and Zambia and the railway workers of Tanganyika (Tanzania) formed an economic elite, cut off from the bulk of the rural population. "The growing sense that the towns were being given preference over the rural areas" was evident, according to one visitor to Africa, as early as the 1950s.

Rural poverty and a population explosion

intensified the drift to the towns, where urban employment opportunities failed to keep pace with migration. Sprawling shanty towns proliferated in most African cities by the 1960s and street corners became the haunts of crowds of unemployed youths.

Such legacies of colonialism were difficult to rectify. Some African governments saw the solution in the rapid development of a modern industrial economy. Large-scale projects such as Ghana's Volta Dam and bauxite-smelting plant, completed in 1965, were impressive achievements, but brought immediate benefits only to a privileged few and tended to widen the gap between prosperous industrial workers and the poverty-stricken rural masses. The apparent prosperity of the Ivory Coast, which had an above-average per capita income of £66 per annum in 1970, hid a growing gulf between urban and rural populations. Official government figures estimated the difference in earnings to be in the ratio of 12:1. In 1963 Nkrumah identified a further danger of rapid industrialization. A shortage of African technical expertise meant that much African industry was still run by foreign companies and the profits were exported to Europe or the United States. Nkrumah called this process "Neo-colonialism":

Immense profits have been and still are being taken out of Africa. Important mineral deposits in various parts of Africa have attracted foreign capital, which has been used mainly to enrich alien investors . . . . The process is still going on, even in the independent countries.

THE MANY AND THE FEW

The gap between rich and poor has been widened by the propensity of political and professional men to inherit the expectations and standard of living of the former colonial rulers. Nkrumah of Ghana and Houphouet-Boigny of the Ivory Coast are examples of leaders who grew away from their people by the opulence of their lifestyles. A correspondent for the newspaper *West African* has described the presidential palace in Abidjan, Ivory Coast:

Nothing is missing; from chandeliers and antique-style furniture in subtly contrasted colours to embossed chinaware and cutlery for over 1,000 guests and a single table that seats hundreds.

RIVALRIES BETWEEN AFRICAN STATES

At the 1977 Organization of African Unity summit at Libreville, the President of Congo-Brazzaville claimed that there were 15 OAU members at present engaged in border conflicts, which were "a legacy of arbitrary border drawing in colonial days". Where state boundaries cut across tribal ones there was bound to be sympathy for fellow tribesmen under alien rule. Between 1974 and 1978 Somalia fought Ethiopia in defence of the Somalis of the Ogaden, who sought to free

themselves from Ethiopian rule. A similar border dispute erupted between Morocco and Algeria in 1963. Other inter-African wars were fought on ideological grounds — to eliminate a regime in a neighbouring state that was thought repugnant. The 1977 Egypt-Libya war or the 1979 overthrow of Idi Amin's dictatorship in Uganda by Tanzanian troops are examples of this type of war.

THE FAILURE OF DEMOCRACY

Faced with economic difficulties, many African leaders resented the time wasted in the democratic process and saw opposition parties as divisive and obstructive. In 1972 Kaunda justified the creation of a one-party state in Zambia:

One party democracy will help us to weed out political opportunists and people who have become expert at manufacturing lies and pretending to oppose what they inwardly welcome . . . . There are no good grounds for organized parliamentary opposition in the country. We can deal with all our problems within the same family.

By the early 1970s multi-party democracy survived nowhere on the African continent. The resumption of party activity in Ghana in 1969 lasted only until 1972, when Dr Busia's government was overthrown by Colonel Acheampong.

One-party or one-man rule, however, was often no less corrupt or inefficient than parliamentary democracy. Nkrumah, Kenyatta, Obote, Haile Selassie, King Farouk, etc, were all accused by their opponents of amassing private fortunes from public office. A Nigerian writer claimed that in his country "a small privileged group lives in comfort and even luxury. They enjoy the fruits of office and make fortunes through their association with foreign business and other interests". Few all-powerful leaders would tolerate criticism. In 1975 a Kenyan politician, Karuiki, was found murdered. He had castigated Kenyatta's accumulation of wealth and power. A parliamentary select committee produced evidence that implicated the government's special police in the murder.

43 Members of the MPLA's army in Angola, with Soviet-supplied weapons. The MPLA has received much aid from the USSR, and several hundred Cuban volunteers have also been reported to be fighting with them.

THE ARMY

Where squabbling parties made efficient government impossible, or where one-party rule resulted in corruption and dictatorship, the army has often intervened as the restorer of national unity or as an anti-corruption agency. Egypt (1952), Congo (1960 and 1965), Algeria (1965), Nigeria (1966), Ghana (1966 and 1972), Central African Republic (1967), Libya (1969), Uganda (1971), Ethiopia (1974) and Dahomey (many times) are among the states that have experienced military rule. The quality of military rulers varied enormously — from the self-effacing and honest Gowon of Nigeria to the cruelly dictatorial Bokassa of the Central African Republic (who had himself declared Emperor Bokassa I in January 1978) and Amin of Uganda.

◁ 42 President Kaunda of Zambia.

AFRICA AND THE COLD WAR

Both East and West sought to turn African disputes to their advantage. The Soviet Union gave military aid to Lumumba in the Congo against the breakaway province of Katanga; while the Somalis and the Ethiopians were supported by the USA and USSR respectively. In May 1978 President Carter of the United States accused the Soviet Union of having instigated the 1978 attempt of Shaba Province to secede from Zaire.

On the whole, however, western fears of growing communist influence in post-independence Africa have not been justified. Most African leaders have followed a policy of non-alignment. They accept aid from whoever offers it, without committing themselves to either side in the Cold War. In 1958 Sekou Touré of Guinea accepted Soviet aid to rebuild the economy shattered by the French departure; three years later the Soviet ambassador was expelled for interfering too much in Guinea's domestic affairs. In 1965 Presidents Nyerere and

Kaunda received Chinese aid to construct the Tanzam railway linking landlocked Zambia with the sea. In the same year Nyerere accepted aid for a road-building programme from Sweden and Canada.

The Cuban presence in Angola since 1975 and the close links between the Soviet Union and the post-1974 military regime in Ethiopia may prove to be exceptions to the rule of non-alignment, although it is too soon to predict how permanent the foreign communist presence will be.

LIBERATION MOVEMENTS

If the tiny Spanish territories and French Somaliland are excluded, by 1968 the only non-independent African states were those where a white minority government resisted majority rule. These included Southern Rhodesia, South West Africa and the three Portuguese colonies. (South Africa was, of course, an independent republic, but her African inhabitants had less political power than under most colonial regimes.) In these areas independence would be gained only by force, not by persuasion. Robert Mugabe, leader of the Popular Front for the Liberation of Zimbabwe (the old African name for Rhodesia) said in an interview in spring 1979:

There was the whole history of our having tried non-violent methods. They had failed completely, and neither the settler regime, nor Britain heeded our cries, they just wouldn't move, they wouldn't yield an inch. So we decided, without any qualms about it, that armed struggle would be the right thing.

African liberation movements operated from centres of friendly neighbouring states. The main centres were Dar es Salaam and (after 1975) Lourenzo Marques (renamed Maputo). The Portuguese colonies were successfully liberated in the 1970s (see page 83), and in 1980 the Zimbabwe guerillas became the legal government of Southern Rhodesia. The South West Africa Peoples Organization (SWAPO) still continues the struggle. Liberation movements have been as subject to tribal and ideological splits as independent African states. The independence of Angola in 1975 was followed by a civil war between three contending factions within the Angolan Liberation Movement — the Marxist MPLA and the non-Marxist UNITA and FNLA. In 1973 rivalries within the Mozambique liberation movement, FRELIMO led to the assassination of leader Mondlane.

THE SEARCH FOR IDENTITY

In 1976 a Ghanaian military leader told a *Times* correspondent that the country was still searching for the type of government best suited to Ghana's circumstances. "This would take a long time, and in the end it would be based on local realities and local experience". Whether it be with Nyerere's "African socialism", Kaunda's "Humanism" or Gaddafi's "Islamic state", African leaders have rejected imported political and economic models and are searching for their own system.

This can be seen most clearly, if also most superficially, in the rejection of names "imposed upon us by the colonialists" (as President Kerekou of Dahomey said on the occasion of the renaming of his state as Benin), and their replacement by names rooted in African history and culture (see page 90). In 1971 the Congo was renamed Zaire; its capital, Leopoldville, became Kinshasa; and Katanga became Shaba. President Mobutu himself changed his Christian names from Joseph-Desiré to the traditional African ones of Sese Seko. With the advent of majority rule in Rhodesia in 1980, the new state reverted to its ancient African name of Zimbabwe.

44   Robert Mugabe.

YOUNG HISTORIAN

A

1   What is "tribalism" and how can it affect the stability of African states?
2   What do you understand by "Africanization"? Why should it have been so popular a policy in the 1960s?
3   What are the economic problems faced by (a) underdeveloped, (b) wealthy African states?
4   What is "urbanization"? What are its disadvantages for (a) rural inhabitants, (b) urban inhabitants?
5   Why has democracy proved such a failure in Africa?
6   What evidence is there to support accusations of increasing Soviet interference in Africa?
7   Why did violent liberation movements emerge?

B

Compose the letters which might have been sent by:
1   An educated African, expressing his hopes and fears for the future of his country after independence.
2   The same African fifteen years later, surveying the developments of the intervening years.
3   A rural African, visiting the town for the first time.
4   An opposition politician in Kenya, on the declaration of a one-party state.
5   A guerilla fighter of the Zimbabwe Liberation Front, justifying the use of force against the white Rhodesian regime.

C

Write propaganda leaflets which might have been issued by the following:
1   The Ghanaian government;
2   An African nationalist;
3   The publicity officer for a liberation movement.

D

Compile a list of the changes of name that have occurred in Africa since independence. Why have such changes taken place?

THE PROBLEMS OF INDEPENDENCE II

ALGERIA

Independent Algeria was faced with the following problems: a high birth-rate (by 1970 the population had reached 16 million); the departure of skilled Europeans; rural under-development; and a drift to the towns which by 1970 had led to a figure of 3 million unemployed or underemployed Muslims. Oil and natural gas accounted for half of Algeria's exports by 1970, bringing unexpected prosperity to a section of the economy and leaving rural poverty untouched.

In 1962, at the start of negotiations with de Gaulle over the terms of Algerian independence, the FLN declared: "The Algerian workers are . . . fighting in order to guarantee land for the peasant, work for the worker and better living conditions." True to this declaration, President Ben Bella initiated sweeping socialist reforms, and proclaimed himself leader of the African independence movement. He planned to hold the second non-aligned conference in Algiers in 1965, but the proposed meeting never took place. In the same year Ben Bella was deposed by the army under Colonel Houari Boumedienne who then ruled Algeria until his death in 1978.

The Algerian army coup which deposed Ben Bella differed in its motive from those which occurred elsewhere in Africa. Boumedienne sought a *less* radical regime and, as President, he severely curtailed the redistribution of land that had started under his predecessor. While oil revenues rose sharply, rural poverty continued and agricultural figures showing low productivity were published in 1975. Many Algerians, especially among the student population, remained loyal to the ideals of Ben Bella, and plots against Boumedienne's life were common. All opposition, however, was severely crushed and the President died peacefully in bed.

TUNISIA AND MOROCCO

In both Tunisia and Morocco the regime established at independence is still maintained today. Bourguiba declared himself President of Tunisia for life in 1974, and Hassan II succeeded his father in Morocco in 1962. Rural poverty and urban unemployment have meant that opposition has not been absent in either state, but in both all dissent is severely repressed. In 1972 a section of the airforce attempted to overthrow Hassan; in January 1978 a general strike in Tunis erupted into violent demonstrations in favour of free speech and the right to form political parties.

EGYPT

Nasser ruled, without significant opposition, until his death in 1970. He introduced a socialist economy, in which land was redistributed to poor farmers, the incomes of the wealthy were limited, and progress was made in both primary and secondary education. In order to reduce Egypt's dependence on the export of cotton, a campaign was started to achieve self-sufficiency in rice cultivation, and large-scale industrial

45   President Habib Bourguiba of Tunisia.

projects were initiated, of which the hydro-electric plant on the Aswan Dam is the most famous. Foreign-owned banks and companies and the Suez Canal were nationalized (see page 45).

Economic progress was hampered, however, by an ambitious foreign policy. Nasser saw himself as the leader of the Arab struggle against Israel, and participated in the Arab-Israeli wars of 1956 and 1967. In order to meet his military needs and to finance industrialization, Nasser accepted massive Soviet aid and accumulated large debts, although he publicly maintained his non-aligned position and refused to allow a communist party to operate in Egypt itself.

Nasser's successor, Anwar Sadat, inherited the results of Nasser's extravagance. The debts incurred in the four wars since 1948 (the fourth was in 1973) led to severe price rises in January 1975 and June 1977, which provoked serious rioting in the major cities. On the second occasion at least seventy-nine people died, and Sadat was forced to cancel the price rises and appeal to other Arab states for financial aid.

Moves towards liberalization and a multi-party state were obstructed by public discontent, and Sadat continued to rule as autocratically as his predecessor. However, between 1977 and 1979 Sadat negotiated a peace treaty with Israel; whether Egypt's defence budget can now be cut sufficiently to allow a significant increase in the standard of living has still to be seen.

LIBYA

At first, the conversion of Libya from a poor to an oil-rich nation did little to improve living standards for the bulk of the population. In fact, the resulting inflation increased the gap between rich and poor. However, oil did provide Libya with the opportunity to lessen its dependence on western aid. The government's failure to take advantage of this opportunity led to the overthrow in 1969 of the pro-western King Idris by a group of young army officers led by Colonel Gaddafi. Gaddafi established himself as the most militant anti-western Arab leader. In 1970 he nationalized all foreign assets, and in the same year Italian settlers were expelled. In April 1973 Gaddafi announced a "cultural revolution", which was aimed at establishing a state based on Islamic principles as laid down in the Koran. All foreign books, "which make our youth increasingly sick", said Gaddafi, were burnt. Libya has remained one of the most intransigent supporters of ever-higher oil-prices for the western world.

ETHIOPIA

Although Haile Selassie made himself a leading advocate of African liberation and unity, by 1970 his domestic regime had become unpopular among young intellectuals. The speed of the reforms of the 1930s, which included the abolition of slavery and the expansion of education, was not maintained after the restoration of the Emperor in 1941; development was centred on the capital, Addis Ababa, while the rural areas stagnated; 90 per cent of the

46   Haile Selassie of Ethiopia, the last Emperor of Ethiopia.

47 Ethiopian soldiers held prisoner by Eritrean guerillas. Since the fall of Haile Selassie, the tide of war has turned in favour of Ethiopia.

population remained illiterate; and political opportunities for the educated were limited by the Emperor's autocratic method of ruling. Further strains were caused by the long drawn-out rebellions in the Ogaden and Eritrea, where non-Ethiopian peoples sought to free themselves from alien rule (see page 63); by the severe drought of 1973; and by the fall in world prices for Ethiopia's chief exports, coffee and oil seeds.

As early as 1961 an unsuccessful army coup had occurred, led by Colonel Mengistu Neway. At his trial the Colonel claimed:

> Ethiopia has been standing still, while our African brothers are moving ahead in the struggle to overcome poverty. What I did was in the best interests of my country.

In June 1974 the armed forces finally assumed complete control, deposing the aged Haile Selassie in September of the same year. Another Colonel Mengistu eventually emerged as the strong-man of the new regime, which has

ruthlessly purged all its opponents. In one night in December 1974 fifty-nine members of Haile Selassie's family and former government were secretly executed. Close relations were established with the Soviet Union and by the end of 1978, with Soviet aid, Mengistu's government had regained control of Eritrea and the Ogaden, although sovereignty over these areas was still somewhat precarious.

GHANA

Between 1957 and 1966 Nkrumah's rule became increasingly intolerant of criticism. One-party rule in Ghana could be justified. Indeed, under Nkrumah's autocracy, considerable economic progress was made, including the Volta River industrial complex and the new harbour at Tema, and there were less spectacular advances in education and the social services. However, Nkrumah was unable to stem the tide of corruption, and he himself pursued a lifestyle out of touch with the majority of people. Allegations were received in the west of the ill-treatment of political prisoners.

In February 1966 a bloodless army coup led by General Ankrah deposed Nkrumah, to the tune of great public rejoicing. Ankrah's successor, Major Afrifa, arranged the return of Ghana to civilian rule in 1969 under the Prime Ministership of Dr Busia. Multi-party democracy, however, proved as corrupt as Nkrumah's regime and considerably less capable of taking positive economic action. A popular song of the time was entitled "The cars are the same, only the drivers are different". A further military coup brought Colonel Acheampong to power in 1972. He tried to reduce Ghana's dependence on cocoa exports and to encourage self-sufficiency in food production in "Operation Feed Yourself". But corruption continued and in June 1979 Ghana's fourth post-independence military coup brought to power a junior officer, Flight-Lieutenant Jerry Rawlings. Rawlings claimed to have been alienated by graft among senior officers and to be interested in improving life for the man-in-the-street.

48 The life-size statue of Nkrumah was "overthrown" at the time of the military coup in Ghana in February 1966.

NIGERIA

The tribal distrust that had delayed Nigerian independence did not abate. Fearing domination by the more populous Muslim north, Ibo army officers led a coup which overthrew the civilian government in 1966. The Federal Prime Minister, Balewa was killed. An anti-Ibo reaction followed. Ibo officials in the north were massacred and a counter-coup brought to power a northerner, General Gowon. Fearful of further genocide, the Ibos declared their secession from Nigeria as the independent state of Biafra in January 1967. For three years a bloody civil war raged, in which fears of a racial massacre of the Ibos at the hands of the northern-dominated central government prompted the beleaguered Biafrans to fight on, even after the capture of Port Harcourt had severed Biafra's last link with the outside world and inflicted starvation on the civilian population. In 1970 Biafra surrendered, and Nigeria became once again a united nation. The expected reprisals against the Ibos did not occur.

From 1970 military rule continued. Sections of the economy flourished, and by 1973 Nigeria was the world's seventh largest oil producer. However, as in other potentially wealthy African states, the incomes of the bulk of the population remained low. Rising oil production led to inflation, with which only well-paid industrial workers could compete. Corruption remained rife. In July 1975 the port of Lagos was brought to a standstill by the delivery of a consignment of cement which was out of all proportion to Nigeria's needs. It is believed that corrupt politicians ordered the cement in response to massive bribes from foreign companies.

FRENCH WEST AND EQUATORIAL AFRICA

Poverty in resources and one-sided economies dominate the histories of the former French territories. A report on Guinea estimated that:

49 In June 1979 Flight-Lieutenant Jerry Rawlings became Ghana's fourth military ruler since independence.

About 60 per cent of the country ought not to be cultivated . . . . About 30 per cent could be used if proper cultivation and anti-erosion methods were employed. Only about 10 per cent, mostly situated on the coast and in river valleys, is capable of being cultivated without particular precautions.

Even the more prosperous Ivory Coast failed to raise the standard of living for the majority of her citizens (see page 62). Consequently, these states all developed into one-party or military dictatorships. By 1979 Benin had had ten military coups in twenty years.

Perhaps the worst example of military dictatorship may be seen in the career of

50 Emperor Bokassa of the Central African Empire, seated on his eagle throne, at his coronation in 1977.

President (formerly Colonel) Bokassa of the Central African Republic. In 1972 he appointed himself President for life and in December 1977 was crowned Emperor Bokassa I, at a ceremony that swallowed up over half the state's annual revenue.

Inter-tribal civil war began in Chad in 1968 and was still going on in 1980, with Muslim nomadic herdsmen from the north resisting the authority of the southern-based government at Fort Lamy. Racial tension continues today (see page 61).

CONGO (ZAIRE)

Within a month of independence civil war had broken out in the Congo, precipitated by an outbreak of latent racial hatred towards Belgian settlers and by tribal animosities. The African rank and file of the Force Publique mutinied, massacring their white officers and any other Belgians in their path. Tshombe of Katanga took advantage of the ensuing chaos to declare Katanga a separate independent state. Ill-able to afford the loss of copper-rich Katanga, Prime Minister Lumumba appealed to the United Nations for military aid. When the UN army proved insufficiently successful, Lumumba accepted Soviet help, while the west gave much tacit support to Tshombe. By the beginning of 1961 political and military chaos had led to the assassination of Lumumba and the existence of *three* separate governments. By 1963 the United Nations army had brought Katanga back into the Congo by force, but in 1965 political corruption brought to power the army commander, General Mobutu.

Mobutu tolerated little opposition and converted himself into a cult figure. In July 1974 "Mobutuism" replaced Roman Catholicism as the official religion of the now renamed Zaire. Crucifixes in public places were replaced by portraits of the president. In August 1972 the national police force was replaced by a corps of gendarmerie owing loyalty only to Mobutu.

Mobutu's rule, however, brought a degree of stability to Zaire that was difficult to foresee in its first few turbulent years. On the other hand, tribal independence had by no means been completely eliminated by 1979, as was demonstrated by two revolts of Shaba Province in 1977 and 1978 (see page 60-1).

76

TANZANIA (TANGANYIKA)

In 1964 Tanganyika was united with Zanzibar and renamed Tanzania; Nyerere remained President.

After 1960 Tanzania faced the common problems of an underdeveloped economy: over-dependence on the world market price for a few staple exports; and demands for economic privileges from a few favourably placed workers such as the railway workers.

In 1967 Nyerere declared a radical solution in the Arusha Declaration, which outlined an aim for greater self-sufficiency in food production and a higher standard of living in the rural areas. This could only be achieved through cooperation between all Tanzanians and sacrifices by urban workers. A system of Ujamaa villages was set up, in which plots were communally owned and profits and labour were shared equally. Nyerere also proposed a new system of education which would prepare Tanzanians for a cooperative rural life, rather than produce an urban elite. In order to set an example of involvement at all levels of the community, government ministers were ordered to give up all business dealings and to limit their incomes. Nyerere himself sold his house in Dar es Salaam.

In a 1977 document entitled "The Arusha Declaration 10 Years After" Nyerere summarized the achievements and failures of his plan:

There are still great inequalities between citizens. A life of poverty is still the experience of the majority of our citizens . . . . Our nation is still economically dependent on the vagaries of the weather and upon economic and political decisions taken by other peoples without our participation or consent.

But he pointed to several positive achievements:

First and foremost we in Tanzania have stopped and reversed a national drift towards the growth of a class society, based on ever-increasing inequality and the exploitation of many for the benefit of the few.

Nyerere adopted a principled stand as an

51 President Nyerere of Tanzania, chaired by supporters, after being returned as President in October 1965 by 96 per cent of the electorate.

opponent of white racialist regimes, and as a supporter of liberation movements. FRELIMO and ZAPU made their headquarters in Dar es Salaam. And it was when Tanzania threatened to leave the Commonwealth — "We are forced to say that to vote South Africa in is to vote us out" — that South Africa was expelled in 1961. Within Tanzania itself, Nyerere made a determined, if not always successful, stand against black racialism (see page 61).

KENYA

Macmillan's prediction that Kenya would "prove another Congo" (see page 53) proved over-pessimistic, although tribal rivalries forced President Kenyatta into an ever-more restrictive dictatorship. In October 1969 former Vice-President, Oginga Odinga, who had formed a breakaway party, the Kenya Peoples Union, in 1966, was placed under house arrest and his party banned. Kenyatta accused Odinga of being "increasingly responsible for the deliberate fomenting of inter-tribal strife".

Kenya's agriculture showed a sound success. According to official figures published in 1973, Kenya's gross national product had increased by 27 per cent since independence. However, as elsewhere, a population increase (3.3 per cent in 1972) had led to unemployment, and inequalities in the standard of living remained large. Protests against this were particularly bitter because of the ostentatious lifestyle enjoyed by government ministers and by Kenyatta himself. In 1973 a proposal to freeze high-level salaries was rejected.

Interesting and encouraging features of the Kenyan scene are the ease with which the white settlers accepted the African government and their loyalty towards the new Kenyan state. The once-feared Kenyatta was known affectionately by his death as the "Old Man".

In spite of tribal dissension, the unity of the country survived Kenyatta's death in 1978, under former Vice-President Daniel Moi.

77

UGANDA

Two serious political crises shook Uganda after 1963. In 1966 Obote's army, led by Colonel Idi Amin, stormed the Kabaka's palace and drove Kabaka Frederick Mutesa — King Freddie — into exile. Buganda's special status, which had caused much jealousy among other tribes, was annulled. Obote himself, however, came under increasing criticism for extravagance and tribal favouritism, and in June 1971 he was over-thrown by a military coup led by Amin, whose Kakua tribe resented the influence wielded by Obote's Kithskin.

Amin's regime soon deteriorated into a reign of tribal and racial terror. Members of the rival Ankoli and Langi tribes suffered in particular. All opposition was suppressed. In September 1977 a former Ugandan minister, then in exile, claimed that for the people of Uganda there was "no known code of conduct that can guarantee personal safety from unwarranted arrest, torture and murder" as "fear engulfs everyone, high and low". In 1972 all non-citizen Asians were precipitately expelled and their property confiscated. *Time* magazine described the Ugandan economy by 1975 as a "shambles".

In February 1979 Ugandan exiles, supported by the Tanzanian army, invaded Uganda. By April Amin had fled to Libya and Kampala was under the control of a government led by Dr Lule and backed by Tanzania. Lule announced his immediate intention to restore the rule of law to Uganda and to rectify the economic situation. However, within two months the Lule government was in disgrace, and the future of Uganda remained uncertain.

ZAMBIA AND MALAWI

From 1964 both Zambia and Malawi gradually became one-party states, in which Kaunda and Banda retained power. Both continued to be worried by tribal divisions.

In Zambia in 1968 Kaunda went so far as to threaten resignation if the politicians did not forget their tribal rivalries and concentrate on

national unity. In October 1972 former Zambian Vice-President, Simon Kapepwe's breakaway party was banned. And, as in Malawi, Jehovah's Witnesses, whom Banda charged with being a "danger to the good government of the state", were outlawed.

In order to spread the benefits of Zambia's copper wealth more evenly, Kaunda adopted a policy of "Humanism", with the aim of re-directing wealth. Kaunda stated in 1965:

A constant preoccupation of my Government is the disparity in the standard of living between the rural masses and the compara-tively limited urban and industrial sector.

In 1973 a code of conduct for ministers was issued, similar to that of neighbouring Tanzania.

Zambia's economic progress was hampered, however, by Kaunda's refusal after 1965 to use the export routes through Rhodesia and Mozambique. New routes such as the Tanzam railway were developed at great cost, and money had to be redirected from urgent development projects. A further blow came in July 1968 when Britain cut off aid to Zambia after the Zambian High Commissioner in London had accused Britain of behaving like a "toothless bulldog" over the UDI issue. Like all developing economies, Zambia is vulnerable to climate upsets; the need to import maize after a period of drought has several times seriously weakened Zambia's foreign exchange reserves.

A further problem was the presence on Zambian soil of Nkomo's faction of the Zimbabwe Liberation Front. On 14 April 1979 Rhodesian soldiers raided Lusaka, the Zambian capital, and burnt the bungalow used as an office by Nkomo. At the 1979 Commonwealth Prime Ministers Conference held in Lusaka great pressure was put on Britain to settle the Rhodesian problem once and for all.

Poorer in economic resources and with a smaller population than Zambia, Malawi sought economic survival by a policy of cooperation with her powerful South African and Rhodesian neighbours. Incomes earned by Malawan labourers in South Africa's flourishing industries are essential for the tiny state's prosperity. Because of this dependence, Banda refused to share Kaunda's support for the Zimbabwe guerillas or to support United Nations sanctions against South Africa. Political objections to this policy within Malawi itself are effectively stifled by the one-party system.

RHODESIA

After UDI Southern Rhodesia was known simply as Rhodesia.

The United Nations placed economic sanctions on Rhodesia after UDI, but these proved insufficiently stringent to destroy Ian Smith's regime. Attempts to negotiate a settlement of the dispute (on HMS *Tiger* in December 1966 and HMS *Fearless* in October 1968) floundered on Smith's refusal and Britain's insistence that safeguards must be written into any constitution for an independent Rhodesia, ensuring steady progress towards majority rule. In 1970 a new conservative government in Britain offered proposals that excluded the safeguard clauses, but implementation was made dependent on approval by the African population. A commission under Lord Pearce visited Rhodesia early in 1972 and was impressed by African opposition to the proposals. A new

African political party, the African National Congress, was founded by a Methodist bishop, Abel Muzorewa, expressly to explain to the black population "the dangers and implications of the proposals".

Within Rhodesia itself, UDI led to an intensification of apartheid and repression. In 1972 pass laws were tightened, so that all Africans were required — under penalty of a fine of 100 Rhodesian dollars (£50) or one year's imprisonment or both — to carry valid identity documents at all times. Outspoken journalists, such as Peter Niesewand, were imprisoned or expelled. Multi-racial institutions, including the famous Cold Comfort Farm, were closed down.

A split within the Rhodesian nationalist movement fulfilled Nkomo's prediction of 1962 that violent movements would develop (see page 55). Muzorewa and Sithole continued to seek a peaceful road to majority rule, while Nkomo and Mugabe opted for guerilla warfare inside Rhodesia as the only effective means of pressure.

Under pressure from increasing terrorism, and prodded by the United States, in 1977 Ian

53 Rhodesia 1978. A black "nanny" oversees her employer's rifle and his child's crib. After guerilla warfare broke out in Rhodesia, white farmers in rural areas were seldom unarmed.

54 Election posters in Rhodesia, April 1979. This was the first election to be held on the basis of one-man rule. ▷

Smith announced his conversion to the principle of majority rule. In April 1979 the first-ever one-man, one-vote elections were held in Rhodesia and Bishop Muzorewa became Prime Minister. However, white Rhodesians retained a guaranteed number of cabinet posts and continued to control the army and police.

At first Mugabe and Nkomo rejected the settlement as a bogus one, asserting that the white population of Rhodesia would never voluntarily relinquish power. However, in the autumn of 1979, under British sponsorship, agreement on a new constitution was reached between Muzorewa's government, white politicians and guerilla leaders. The elections of March 1980 produced a substantial majority for the Mugabe faction, the result was accepted by the whites as fair, and in April 1980 Mugabe became the first Prime Minister of the legally independent Zimbabwe. Whether white and black Africans will continue to cooperate in the

development of a genuine multi-racial society remains to be seen.

SOUTH AFRICA

Apartheid and repression continued in South Africa. In 1964 nationalist leader Nelson Mandela was imprisoned for life. In 1969 the Bureau of State Security (BOSS) was founded. Its function was to investigate all matters concerning state security, and it was answerable not to parliament, but only to the ministers. Its activities could therefore easily be kept secret. In September 1977 a black student

55 On 29 May 1979 Bishop Abel Muzorewa (front) was sworn in as Prime Minister by the President at the government house of Rhodesia. Ian Smith (seated behind) was made Minister without Portfolio in Muzorewa's government.

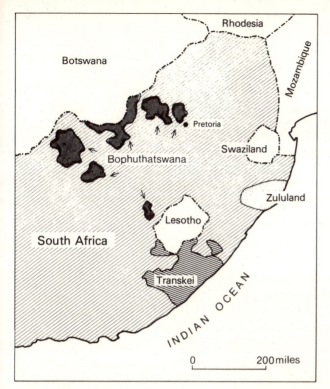

56   The Bantustans.

leader, Steve Biko, died in police custody. The official explanation was that he died after a hunger strike, but a commission of judges placed the blame on police brutality.

By 1979 three Bantustans had been created: Zululand, Transkei and Bophuthatswana. These "homelands" were so poor that they were economically dependent on South Africa and on the wages of migrant workers. However, such circumstances did not turn the Bantustan leaders into mere ciphers. In an interview in the *South African Times* in September 1977 The Transkei ambassador to South Africa warned:

> We are the last negotiating generation. Eventually there will be a spontaneous outburst by the people such as is going on in Soweto. Transkei will find itself in a new mood and moving in a direction no one has anticipated.

African opposition within the Republic of South Africa itself has tended to abandon legal forms and advocate violence instead. In 1977 a proposal to replace Bantu with Afrikaans as the medium of instruction in African schools led to widespread rioting in the township of Soweto outside Johannesburg and a boycott of schools that lasted into 1978.

In foreign policy, South Africa's wish was to preserve her own security. She opened a "dialogue" with friendly or dependent black African states, such as Malawi (still dependent on the wages from migrant labour), Lesotho and the Ivory Coast. In 1975 South African troops intervened unsuccessfully in Angola, in support of the non-Marxist UNITA and FNLA forces.

In spite of the Soweto riots, the outspokenness of the Bantustan leaders and the resignation of President Vorster in 1979 over the Muldergate scandal, involving the misuse of government money, the overthrow of the system in South Africa seemed as far away as ever in 1980. African resistance was still hampered by the dependence of Africans on the white economy.

SOUTH WEST AFRICA (NAMIBIA)

World opinion and the outbreak of African unrest in its fifth state (in 1972 the first major African strike occurred in Ovamboland) persuaded the South African government to grant a form of independence to South West Africa. This was based on separate legislative councils for each racial group, including the white settlers. Apartheid legislation, such as the ban on mixed marriages, was repealed. SWAPO, however, refused to accept the new constitution, claiming that the regime would be a puppet of South Africa; guerilla activity continued.

PORTUGUESE AFRICA

In spite of escalating guerilla activity, few observers even as late as 1970 saw any sign of a breach in Portugal's determination to stay in Africa. This determination was only strengthened by the discovery of oil in Cabinda in northern Angola. A massive hydro-electric project for Mozambique, the Cabora Bassa dam, was begun in conjunction with South Africa and scheduled for completion in 1979.

Anti-Portuguese guerilla movements began in Angola in 1961, in Guinea-Bissau in 1963 and in Mozambique in the late 1960s. Guerilla leaders realized that success would occur only if the liberation movements were supported by

On signs: "No more Christa", "Viva Headmen away with A", "No Round Table Talks We want NAMIBIA", "NO MORE BOER LIES!!", "Stop you GAMES NAMIBIA WILL BE FREE!!", "NO MORE POLICE DOGS!"

57 SWAPO demonstrators against the new South African-sponsored constitution of South West Africa (Namibia).

the local population (this was one of the secrets of Mao Tse-tung's spectacular success in China in the 1930s and '40s). As each area was liberated, guerillas set up a civilian administration. including schools and hospitals. In the words of Guinea leader, Cabral:

> The leaders live day by day with various peasant groups in the heart of the rural populations and come to know the people better . . . . On their side, the working masses and especially the peasants, who are usually illiterate and have never moved outside the boundaries of their village or region come into contact with other groups . . . they break the bonds of the village universe and integrate progressively with their country and with the world.

Success was greatest in Guinea-Bissau, which had liberated itself by 1973. The important turning-point came, however, in 1974, when a revolution in Portugal brought to power the former commander in Guinea, General Spinola. Aware of the extent to which colonial wars were

stretching Portugal's slender resources, Spinola announced in a broadcast on 17 July 1974:

> The moment has come for the President of the Republic to reiterate solemnly our recognition of the rights of the inhabitants of Portugal's overseas territories to self-determination, including the immediate recognition of their right to independence . . . in the end we are celebrating the most difficult of victories . . . victory over ourselves, over our error and over our contradictions.

Mozambique and Angola became independent in 1975, but a peaceful transition was obstructed in Mozambique by white settler opposition and in Angola by a civil war between rival liberation groups. By the end of 1975 the MPLA seemed to be in control in Angola, but in early 1978 it became evident that UNITA guerillas were still active.

YOUNG HISTORIAN

A

1 Why does rural poverty continue in the Maghrib states? What measures have been taken to overcome it in the different states, and how successful have such measures been?

2 What were Nasser's achievements in Egypt? What problems did he leave for his successors?

3 Why did Haile Selassie lose his throne?

4 Why have so many military coups occurred in Ghana and Nigeria? Has either state succeeded in solving the problems that caused these coups?

5 Give an account of 2 civil wars that have occurred in post-independence Africa. What were (a) the causes, (b) the outcome, (c) the methods by which stability was eventually restored?

6 How and with what success have Tanzania and Zambia attempted to overcome their economic problems since independence?

7 How have tribal rivalries affected the development of (a) Kenya, (b) Uganda?

8 Why did it take fifteen years for a settlement to be found for the Rhodesian problem? What problems confront the new state of Zimbabwe?

9 In what ways has South Africa become a police state? Are there any signs of successful opposition to the system?

10 How and why did independence finally come to Portuguese Africa?

B

How might the following have justified their actions:

1 A plotter against Boumedienne.
2 A rioter in Cairo in 1977.
3 Gaddafi.
4 A leader of the 1966 Ghanaian coup.
5 A Biafran in 1967.
6 A Tanzanian soldier in Uganda 1979.
7 Bishop Muzorewa on (a) his opposition to the 1971 proposals, (b) his support for majority rule in 1979.
8 A SWAPO guerilla.
9 General Spinola.

C

Write the headlines which might have appeared above reports on the following events, in (a) a newspaper in the country concerned, (b) a European newspaper:

1 Sadat's peace treaty with Israel.
2 Gaddafi's cultural revolution.
3 The overthrow of Haile Selassie.
4 The overthrow of Nkrumah.
5 The crowning of Bokassa.
6 The death of Kenyatta.
7 The opening of the Tanzam railway.
8 The death of Steve Biko.

D

1 Design a propaganda poster for an Ujamaa village.
2 Design a poster in support of the Nigerian Federal government during the civil war.
3 Design an advertisement, issued by the South African government, urging participation in the Namibian elections.

THE SEARCH FOR UNITY

THE NEED FOR UNITY

Economic and tribal difficulties experienced by African states could well be eased by a greater degree of unity between groups of states. The abolition of customs duties, joint financing of expensive projects, a pooling of resources (Nkrumah dreamt of a union of Nigerian oil, Ghanaian electricity and Guinean bauxite), and the avoidance of debilitating border disputes are all possible advantages to be gained from regional unions.

Moreover, there is also a case to be made for some form of international organization covering the whole continent, if Africa desires to present to the world a common front on such problems as South Africa, Rhodesia and the Cold War, and if she wishes to find a means of settling internal disputes without inviting foreign interference. It was in this spirit that the Organization of African Unity (OAU) was founded in 1963.

REGIONAL UNIONS

There have been several attempted unions between two or more neighbouring states, but apart from the 1964 Tanganyika/Zanzibar union, none have been permanently successful. Unions that have failed include the creation of a "Greater Arab Maghrib", proposed in 1964 at Tangier; a union between Egypt and Libya in 1977; and the idea of an East African Union, proposed by Nyerere before independence. Indeed, since independence, cooperation between African states has to some extent declined. Kenya, Uganda and Tanzania inherited both the East African Common Services Authority, which provided a common airline, railway, postal and telephone service, and PAFMECA, the Pan-African Freedom Movement for East and Central Africa. By 1978 the entire structure lay in ruins.

The reasons for the failure of regional unions are many and vary from case to case. Two frequent causes, however, are the existence of touchy national pride in newly independent states and ideological differences. The final disintegration of the East African Union was precipitated by Tanzania's distaste for the Amin regime. The proposed Egyptian-Libyan union floundered on Gaddafi's accusation that Egypt was not a sufficiently fervent Islamic state. Differences between Morocco, Algeria, Libya and Tunisia, over their respective devotion to Islam and hostility to the western world, sabotaged plans for a Greater Arab Maghrib.

This does not mean that examples of unselfish cooperation have not occurred. Among these are the aid given by Tanzania to Zambia in re-routing her trade after UDI and the £100,000,000 loan granted by Ghana to Guinea after French withdrawal in 1958. In 1975 ECOWAS, the Economic Community of West African States (a sort of West African Common Market) was founded.

ORGANIZATION OF AFRICAN UNITY

Nkrumah advocated a policy of *Pan-Africanism*. Africans were a common people with a common

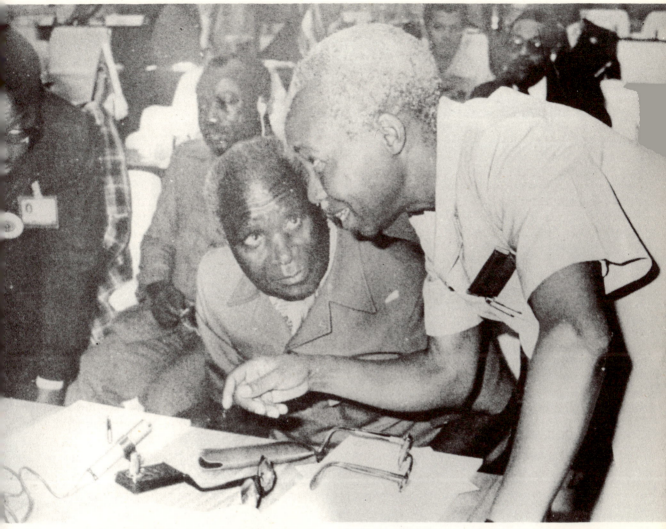

58 Tanzanian President Dr Julius Nyerere leaves his
seat to discuss a point with the Zambian President
Kenneth Kaunda at a summit of the Organization of
African Unity in Khartoum. The OAU's effectiveness is
hampered by deep differences of opinion between
African leaders.

cultural heritage of which they should be proud.
It was therefore in the interests of all Africans to
act in total unity, in order to defend their way
of life against outside interference.

In 1963 the OAU was established in Addis
Ababa. Heads of State meet once a year at
summit conferences and a permanent secretariat
sits in the Ethiopian capital to deal with day-to-
day formation and execution of policy. The
OAU, however, fell far short of Nkrumah's ideal.
It did not provide a common government for
Africa, and each state retains full independence

and freedom of action. When the Ghanaian
leader suggested a pan-African government, the
Nigerian Prime Minister recoiled in horror:

A United States of Africa? Oh, surely it is
very premature to start talking about any-
thing like that. Nigeria has not the slightest
intention of surrendering her sovereignty,
as soon as she gained her independence, to
anyone else, including other West African
countries.

There were many other statesmen who shared
Balewa's view. The OAU's only method of
action is to inspire *voluntary* cooperation on
matters of common concern.

There have been some successes. The
Committee for Liberation, with its headquarters
at Dar es Salaam, has granted crucial aid to the

guerilla movements in the Portuguese territories and South Africa. Some potentially explosive border disputes have been solved. At the 1967 Kinshasa meeting the frontier dispute between Somalia and Kenya was successfully settled. The OAU insistence that the Nigerian civil was was purely an African problem did much to discourage the intervention of the superpowers.

However, OAU effectiveness is often hampered by differences of opinion among its members. The OAU's official policy support for the Nigerian Federal government during that country's civil war was defied by Tanzania, Zambia, Gabon and the Ivory Coast — all of whom recognized Biafra. In December 1966 Malawi and Lesotho refused to implement sanctions against Rhodesia. The OAU has also split over the civil war in Angola, the rebellion of Shaba and over Uganda. The latter issue sparked off a personal confrontation between Gaddafi of Libya and King Hassan of Morocco. The greatest subject of dispute, however, is South Africa. A common black African front, in condemning apartheid and the continuing occupation of South West Africa, has been breached by Malawi, Lesotho and the Ivory Coast, who have responded to South African offers of "Dialogue" in exchange for economic aid.

Perhaps the greatest weakness of the OAU is its inability to enforce its verdicts. Paper reconciliations, such as those between Ethiopia and Somalia, and Tanzania and Uganda, at the 1973 summit, proved ineffective in the face of the continuing conflict of interests between the states concerned.

AFRICA AT THE UNITED NATIONS

In spite of their divisions, African states have been able to present a common front on a number of problems at the United Nations and have introduced some new issues. Resolutions condemning South Africa and Rhodesia and calling for the independence of Namibia and the Portuguese territories succeeded in drawing the attention of the world to these issues. Before China's admission to the United Nations in 1973, all black African states voted consistently for a lifting of the American veto on China's entry.

Within the Commonwealth African pressure caused the expulsion of South Africa, a moderation of British arms sales to South Africa, and it may well have stiffened Britain's determination to maintain economic sanctions against Rhodesia.

YOUNG HISTORIAN

A

1 What advantages might be gained from (a) regional unions, (b) a super-national government in Africa?
2 Give specific examples of regional unions that have failed.
3 What are the major differences between the OAU and Nkrumah's dream of a Pan-African government? Why does the OAU find it so difficult to settle disputes?
4 What important issues still divide African states?

B

1 Write a broadsheet by a Pan-African stressing the advantages to Africa of his doctrine.
2 Compose the letter which might have been written by Nyerere, justifying his demolition of the East African Community in the 1970s.

CONCLUSION - THE UNANSWERED QUESTIONS

The years since the start of the decolonization process in the mid 1950s mark the beginning of the African struggle for prosperity and identity in the modern world. The problems of underdevelopment and the gap between rich and poor, of tribal divisions and of susceptibility to tyrannical rule still continue. The motives given by the instigators of the 1979 military coup in Ghana were the same as those given by Ankrah thirteen years before — corrupt leaders whose opulent lifestyles put them out of touch with the majority of the population. It is certainly too early to judge whether Rawlings' government of the "underdog", Nyerere's continued insistence on the Arusha principles, or FRELIMO's emphasis on peasant participation in economic and political planning, will succeed in creating new social forms which are capable of solving many of Africa's problems.

The thorny problem of South Africa remains. It is difficult to envisage any fundamental change in that country's political system unless it is brought about by African violence.

Growing Soviet and Cuban involvement in Angola and Ethiopia has increased the danger of Africa's becoming a battleground in the Cold War.

There are, however, some grounds for optimism. The strangle-hold over western economies of oil-producing countries such as Nigeria, Algeria and Libya has vastly increased the potential incomes of these states. It is up to them to see that this wealth is used constructively to improve the living standards of all the population. The peaceful transfer of power in Kenya after Kenyatta's death, the restrained behaviour of the Tanzanian army in Uganda in the spring of 1979, and the courage of President Sadat in reversing the thirty-year old Egyptian policy of hostility towards Israel are all promising signs of a growing political maturity.

There are no conclusions to the problems of Africa, only unanswered and, as yet unanswerable, questions.

LIST OF DATES OF INDEPENDENCE

State	Date of Independence	Change of Name	Capital
South Africa	already independent	Republic of South Africa 1961	Pretoria (seat of government)
Ethiopia	already independent		Addis Ababa
Liberia	already independent		Monrovia
Libya	1950		Tripoli & Benghazi
Egypt	Formal independence 1936. Withdrawal of foreign troops 1956		Cairo
Sudan	1956		Khartoum
Morocco	1956		Rabat
Tunisia	1956		Tunis
Gold Coast	1957	Ghana 1957	Accra
Guinea (formerly part of French West Africa)	1958		Conakry
French West Africa, as the separate republics of:	1960		
Dahomey		Benin	Cotonou
Soudan		Mali 1960	Bamako
Mauritania			Nouakchott
Niger			Niamey
Ivory Coast			Abidjan
Senegal			Dakar
Upper Volta			Ouagadougou
Togo			Lomé
Cameroons		Cameroun	Yaounde

French Equatorial Africa as independent republics of:	1960		
Oubangui-Chari		Central African Republic	Bangui
Chad			Fort Lamy
Congo-Moyen		Congo-Brazzaville	Brazzaville
Gabon			Libreville
Madagascar	1960	Malagasy Republic	Tananarive
Nigeria	1960		Lagos
Somalia (union of British and Italian Somalilands)	1960		Mogadishu
Congo	1960	Zaire	Kinshasa
Tanganyika	1961	Tanzania 1964	Dar es Salaam
Sierra Leone	1961		Freetown
Algeria	1962		Algiers
Urundi	1962	Burundi	
Ruanda	1962	Rwanda	
Uganda	1962		Kampala
Zanzibar	1963	Tanzania (1964 union with Tanganyika)	Zanzibar
Kenya	1963		Nairobi
Nyasaland	1964	Malawi	Lilongwe
Northern Rhodesia	1964	Zambia	Lusaka
The Gambia	1965		Bathurst
Bechuanaland	1966	Botswana	Gaberones
Basutoland	1966	Lesotho	Maseru
Swaziland	1967		Mbabane
Spanish Guinea	1968	Equatorial Guinea 1968	Bata
Mauritius	1969		Réunion
Guinea-Bissau	1973		Bissau
Angola	1975		Luanda
Mozambique	1975		Lourenzo-Marques (1976 Maputo)
Spanish Sahara	1976	Saharan Arab Republic	Villa Cisneros & Samra
Rhodesia	1980	Zimbabwe	Salisbury

Territories whose status is still in dispute

South West Africa (Namibia)			Windhoek

GLOSSARY

Afrikaner	South African of Dutch descent.
Africanization	Policy of replacing European or Asian personnel with native-born Africans.
ANC	(a) African National Congress, an opposition movement in South Africa, founded in 1912 and now banned; (b) African National Council, formed by Bishop Muzorewa in 1972, to oppose British proposals for a settlement with Ian Smith's government.
Apartheid	South African system of complete separation of races. Africans are to be rehoused in tribal homelands or "Bantustans". Where total physical separation is impossible, apartheid refers to the provision of separate facilities for blacks and whites.
Bantustan	African "homeland", established under South African apartheid legislation.
Bedouin	Collective name given to the nomadic tribes of the Sahara.
Berbers	Another collective name for Saharan nomads.
Boer	South African of Dutch descent.
Buganda/Uganda	The colony of Uganda was formed from an amalgamation of the three kingdoms of Buganda, Toro and Bunyoro. Of these, Buganda was the most prominent and dominated Uganda after independence.
Cash-crop economy	A system where one or two profitable crops are grown for export. The profits are then used to import the necessities of life and pay taxes.
Cold Comfort Farm	A multi-racial cooperative farm founded by a white Rhodesian missionary, Guy Clutton-Brock. It aimed to teach not only practical skills, but also the delicate art of racial tolerance.
Colour bar	Exclusion of persons from employment or public utilities on the grounds of race or colour.
Colon	A French settler in Algeria.
Concessionary Company	A company which is given the right, usually for a limited period of time, to exploit the resources of a region in exchange for undertaking certain obligations — for example to maintain law and order.
Coptic Church	A distinct form of Christianity, evolved in Egypt and Ethiopia.
CPP	Convention Peoples Party. Nkrumah's party. Led Ghana to independence.
Emir	Muslim chief.
Fellahin	Egyptian peasants.
FLN	Army of liberation in Algeria 1954-1962.
FNLA	Non-Marxist forces active in Angolan civil war 1975.
FRELIMO	Guerilla movement which fought for the independence of Mozambique.

	Led by Samora Machel. Government of Mozambique since 1975.
Galla	Pagan Negro people of Southern Ethiopia.
Guerillas	Irregular soldiers using tactics of ambush etc, instead of conventional warfare.
Indigena	Non-citizen African in the Portuguese colonies, lacking any protection in law. Status abolished circa 1960.
Indigenat	Law applied to non-citizen Africans in the French colonies, by which colonial officials had the right to imprison without trial.
Istiqlal	Party of independence in Morocco.
Kabaka	Hereditary ruler of Buganda. Head of State of Uganda, 1963-1966.
KANU	Kenyan African National Union. Only legal party in Kenya.
KAPU	Kenyan African Peoples Union. Former opposition party in Kenya. Illegal since 1969.
Khedive	Hereditary ruler of Egypt. In theory, he was subordinate to the Sultan of Turkey; by 1880, however, the Khedive was in effect an independent potentate.
Maghrib	North African coastal area, comprising the modern states of Algeria, Morocco, Libya and Tunisia.
Mandate System	System designed by the League of Nations in 1919, whereby confiscated German colonies were to be governed by the victorious powers, in the interests of the native inhabitants.
Metropolitan France	Mainland France. Term used to distinguish France proper from her overseas territories (France d'Outremer).
MPLA	Marxist party of Angola. In power from 1975.
Namibia	African name for South West Africa.
Neocolonialism	Economic dependence of Africa on the former colonial powers, that exists even after political independence. The term was popularized by Nkrumah.
Neo-Destour	Tunisian party of independence, led by Habib Bourguiba.
Nomads	Peoples with no fixed home, who move their herds from one fertile area to another.
Ogaden	Muslim area in eastern Ethiopia, annexed by Menelik in the 1890s.
Pan-Africanism	A doctrine that stresses the common heritage and interests of all Africans. Urges joint action and a common front on all issues.
Pass Laws	Laws by which Africans are required to carry special passes before entering white areas; an effective means of controlling African freedom of movement. Still in force in South Africa; abandoned in Namibia and Zimbabwe.
Pastoralists	Peoples who live by raising grazing animals. May be settled or nomadic.
Protectorate	Form of colonial government by which a native society accepts foreign rule in return for protection against outside interference.
Resident	This was the title the French used in north Africa (though not elsewhere) instead of "governor".
Rhodesia Front	White supremacist party led by Ian Smith. Led Southern Rhodesia to UDI in 1965.
Rifs	Berbers of Morocco.
Sahel	Savannah area south of the Sahara, comprising the modern states of Mauritania, Mali, Niger, Upper Volta, Senegal, Chad and northern Nigeria.
Sanussi	Berbers of Libya; fanatical Muslims.
Secession	The breaking-away of part of a state to form a new political unit.

Sisal	A substance similar to hemp, used for making strong rope. One of the main exports of Tanzania.
Subjects	Non-citizen Africans in the French colonies.
Subsistence agriculture	Economy in which individual families produce all the goods necessary for their own survival. Usually an economy without trade or money.
TANU	Tanganyika African National Union. The only legal party in mainland Tanzania. Led by Julius Nyerere.
Trusteeship Council	United Nations version of Mandates Commission.
UNITA	Non-Marxist party in Angolan civil war. Guerilla units are still active in Angola.
Veldt	High grasslands of South Africa.
ZAPU	Zimbabwe African Peoples Union. Once led from Zambia by Joshua Nkomo. Instated in 1980 as legal opposition party in new state of Zimbabwe.

INDEX

The numbers in **bold type** refer to figure numbers of the illustrations

94